NATURE'S
STERNEST
PAINTER

NATURE'S STERNEST PAINTER

FIVE ESSAYS ON
THE POETRY OF
GEORGE CRABBE

BY

OLIVER F. SIGWORTH

THE UNIVERSITY OF ARIZONA PRESS
TUCSON · 1965

TO THE MEMORY
OF THREE WHO HELPED:
JAY, BERTHA, ALICE

PREFACE

Yet Truth sometimes will lend her noblest fires
And decorate the verse herself inspires:
This fact in Virtue's name let Crabbe attest;
Though nature's sternest painter, yet the best.

—ENGLISH BARDS AND SCOTCH REVIEWERS

WHATEVER non-literary motives may have inspired Byron's youthful encomium of Crabbe, the fact that the judgment was repeated in the maturity of the romantic poet is not so remarkable as it may seem to those who have read only *The Village*, and that, perhaps, only in anthologized excerpts, for there can be little doubt that Crabbe has been more discussed by professors than read by students, more commended by critics than perused by readers. Crabbe's work, in fact, is somewhat similar to that of Byron in that it must be read in quantity if it is really to be enjoyed in part, and with Crabbe this initial obstacle may be for us in these lazier times a forbidding one, though it may appear more forbidding in the three bulky tomes of the Cambridge edition than it actually turns out to be. But Byron's continued appreciation of his older contemporary was quite in accord with the prevailing taste of his own day, and his concern with "Truth" was one reflecting that taste. Tastes change, and so do truths; yet there is still a taste for Crabbe, as appreciations by Mr. Leavis, Mr. Blunden, and Mr. E. M. Forster will attest, and perhaps the mutation of truth in a century and a half is less than it is convenient for us to believe. That Crabbe may still have something to say to us is sufficiently proved by Mr. Britten's opera *Peter Grimes*.

It is the purpose of these essays, by attempting to illuminate some of the ways in which Crabbe's mind worked, not to defend him against his detractors—for nobody since Saintsbury has bothered to detract from what fame remains to the old gentleman—but to point out some of his great virtues. These he has, and they seem to me virtues which the mid-twentieth century might profitably pause to consider. Crabbe can be comfortable reading, if only because of his good sense, but I hope I have pointed out that his good qualities go far beyond this unexciting norm, which was hardly more normal in his day than in ours.

In composing these studies I have incurred so many debts of so varied a nature that to acknowledge them all would be to enumerate my friends of more years past than I like to think. I wish to thank Mr. Varley H. Lang for permitting me to make use of his unpublished dissertation, "Some Aspects of George Crabbe's Realism," Johns Hopkins, 1938. To Lawrence H. Parks and Richard C. Atkins I owe special debts, and I take particular pleasure in expressing my gratitude to Professor Bertrand H. Bronson. Had I been able even in part to attain the high goals which he set by precept and example this would have been a different book, and a better one.

OLIVER F. SIGWORTH

Tucson, 1965

CONTENTS

1 | CRABBE

AND THE EIGHTEENTH CENTURY

In DECEMBER, 1817, an aging gentleman hurried from London to Trowbridge carrying three thousand pounds in notes. "He must," according to Thomas Moore, "take them with him to Trowbridge, and show them to his son John. They would hardly believe his good luck, at home, if they did not see the bills."[1] The gentleman was George Crabbe, and the three thousand pounds was the payment made to him by his new publisher, John Murray, for *Tales of the Hall* and for the copyrights of his earlier works. But the money was only a symbol of his success, for earlier in the year he had visited London, and through the good offices of Samuel Rogers[2] he had been lavishly entertained by the most illustrious society of the metropolis. The year was the crest of the tide for Crabbe. It marked the first of his several returns to London society after having been absent from the

[1] Quoted by George Crabbe, son of the poet, in *The Life of George Crabbe* (with introduction by E. M. Forster), Oxford World's Classics, London, 1932, p. 254. [Cited hereafter as *Life.*] See also Thomas Moore, *Memoirs* . . . , London, 1853, vol. II, p. 259 for a slightly different version of the anecdote.

[2] He had been introduced to Rogers by William Lisle Bowles, or by Lord Lansdowne, whom he knew through Bowles. See René Huchon, *George Crabbe and his Times, 1754–1832* (tr. from the French by Frederick Clarke, M.A.), London, 1907, p. 391. [Cited hereafter as *Huchon.*]

capital for more than thirty years,[3] and it was easy to believe that he may have been less pleased by the munificent sum he received for his writings than by the sincere admiration he aroused in persons so diverse as Lady Holland, Thomas Campbell, and George Canning. He was naïvely delighted by the money; he was serenely and humbly delighted by his host of new friends.

This society, these friends, were the very ones whom we, today, believe so lamentably to have failed in poetic appreciation when they ostracized Shelley, and ignored Keats; when they appreciated only belatedly the genius of Wordsworth and Coleridge, all the while adulating Campbell, Rogers, Moore, and, indeed, Crabbe. The latter, however, seems to have occupied a special place in their attentions, for he could almost be regarded as the last of a race of fallen giants. Thomas Campbell, in a letter to him, wrote, "I have something of a filial upward-looking affection for your matured genius and patriarchal reputation . . ." and he speaks of "This reverence for your classic name."[4] "Classic" would have seemed less inappropriate in 1817 than it may today, for Crabbe had, after all, known Johnson, had been a friend of Reynolds, and was patronized by Edmund Burke. His first important poem had been published before some of his 1817 friends were born, and he was to survive, his life was to comprehend entirely the lives of Shelley, Keats, and Byron, while Coleridge was to be able to look back no more than two years to the death of Crabbe.

These years from 1783—the year of the publication of *The Village*—to 1817 saw some of the most startling changes in English poetry, as well as English politics, which can be remarked by an historian; yet Crabbe seems to have given little heed either to the one revolution or to the other.[5] His poetry

3 He had taken his wife, as a treat, to London in 1813, but she was in the last stages of her final illness, and the visit was not a social one.

4 Dated July, 1817. See William Beattie (editor), *Life and Letters of Thomas Campbell*, London, 1850, vol. II, p. 329.

5 Mention of "the last King Lewis" occurs in *Parish Register* I, 43; of the Battle of the Nile, *ibid.*, 65–70; and of the Napoleonic Wars, *Tales of the Hall*, VIII, 172. Crabbe's letters to Mary Leadbeater and Elizabeth Charter display a real

develops—and develops with singular consistency and integrity—but we cannot help feeling that it would have done so in very much the same way had there been no French Revolution or Napoleonic Wars, or had the *Lyrical Ballads* never appeared in print.

He did, for the most part, hold himself aloof from the turmoil, from the great changes in direction which the social body was beginning to experience, but, just as a man on a ship, unaware of or not heeding his ultimate destination, might nevertheless observe closely the life in his floating cosmos, so Crabbe was never aloof from the life immediately around him. Quite the opposite. It is the penetration of his records of the men and manners passing under his direct gaze which gives his poetry its highly distinctive flavor, and which makes his created world linger in the memory after some products of more consciously "poetic" art have faded from the mind. It is the fact that his poetry is, in some sense, an objective record of the poet's observations which was enough, in the second decade of the nineteenth century, to demonstrate to the public an affinity of the poet with an earlier age.

Even when the "Romantic Movement" was at its height, Jeffrey and Gifford were there to conserve and cherish, each in his own way, the last drops of diluted Augustan elixir, and while they may have been aware of some "romantic" pollution in the poems of Crabbe, they found him sufficiently pure to be acceptable to their exclusive tastes. His couplets pleased their eye and, usually, their ear; and his subjects, slightly eccentric as his treatment of them may have seemed, were, as we shall see, such as could fit into a taste schooled in eighteenth-century verse. In their judgment the common reader of the time obviously concurred; for the common reader, inevitably conservative, is always displeased by novelty, but comforted by being able to recognize patterns of verse and thought in which he feels at ease.

The instinct of the reviewers and the common reader was right. Crabbe was, in several possible senses of that confused

and sympathetic concern with social problems, but certainly no revolutionary interests. These will be discussed below.

term, an eighteenth-century poet. Born in the middle of the
century, he was educated before revolutions made men doubt
the ideals of the century, and served an important part of his
poetic apprenticeship under the aegis of Edmund Burke who,
although he was at the time something of a Whig, did not let the
Whiggery which Dr. Johnson so deplored impair his judgment
of poetry.

Of Burke himself and of his interest in Crabbe there will be
more to say presently. That interest, however, was aroused not
simply because Crabbe was, as he described himself, "one of
those outcasts on the world, who are without a friend, without
employment, and without bread,"[6] reason though that might
have been. Crabbe's son, in the biography, remarks: "Enlarged
as was Mr. Burke's benevolence, had not the writings which
were submitted to his inspection possessed the marks of real
genius, the applicant would probably have been dismissed with
a little pecuniary assistance. I must add that, even had his poems
been evidently meritorious, it is not to be supposed that the
author would have at once excited the strongest personal interest in such a mind, unless he had, during this interview, exhibited the traits of a pure and worthy character."[7] The poems
Burke saw, without doubt, were possessed of "marks of real
genius," and it is much to Burke's credit that he was able to
perceive these marks beneath layers of amateurish dross.
Genius, we must believe however, does not exist *in vacuo;* nor is
a "pure and worthy character" the product of capricious fortune. These were qualities which the eighteenth century respected, qualities in Crabbe which attracted Burke.[8] It may
interest us, therefore, to speculate upon the roots of some of
these qualities in Crabbe's early life and work.

[6] Crabbe's first letter to Burke, dated 1781. *Huchon,* p. 112, dates it more
specifically as "towards the end of February or the beginning of March," but on
what evidence is not clear. He provides a facsimile of the letter, which is also
quoted in *Life,* p. 86.

[7] *Life,* p. 90.

[8] It is interesting that almost a half-century later Landor was also attracted
by Crabbe's moral character. See the conversation between Southey and Porson,
Imaginary Conversations (ed. Charles Crump), London, 1891, vol. III, p. 216.

2

For Crabbe's life his son's biography is the chief source, and since that delightful book is easily obtainable it is unnecessary to re-tell the whole story here. As Mr. E. M. Forster truly remarks, the son "did present his father's character and not someone else's,"[9] so we may feel free to draw upon the first biography, particularly as it is corrected by M. Huchon, even though it is not, strictly speaking, definitive.

The very term "definitive" would be out of place, for like that of so many authors born beneath the highest station, the early life of George Crabbe is clouded with such considerable obscurity that even the poet's son had not the facts at his command completely to unveil it. We know that he was born on December 24, 1754,[10] in the sea-swept town of Aldborough—or, as it is now spelled, Aldeburgh—on the coast of Suffolk, the eldest of a family of six children. The *pater familias,* according to his son's biographer, had been "originally educated for trade," but appears to have been, "very early in life, the keeper of a parochial school in the porch of the church of Orford."[11] In 1754 he was collector of salt-duties, or Salt-Master, for the port of Aldborough, some fifteen miles to the north. At the time of his first son's birth he was vigorous, skillful in business, and above all intellectually active. The poet's biographer records that the Salt-Master "used, occasionally, to read aloud to his family in the evenings, passages from Milton, Young, or some other of our graver classics, with, as his son thought long afterwards, remarkable judgment, and with powerful effect,"[12] and that he had a considerable predilection for mathematics and an "extraordinary faculty of calculation."[13] Although he was a man

9 *Life,* p. xi.

10 Crabbe's own statement, in a letter to Elizabeth Charter, Nov. 9, 1824. See A. M. Broadley and Walter Jerrold, *The Romance of an Elderly Poet,* London, 1913, p. 272. [Cited hereafter as Broadley and Jerrold.] Huchon was unaware of this document. See his note, p. 7, which Mr. Forster seems to have misread (*Life,* p. xiii).

11 *Life,* p. 4.　　　　12 *Life,* p. 12.　　　　13 *Life,* p. 4.

of "imperious temper and violent passions,"[14] it is likely that Miss Wylie has laid undue stress on the sordidness of Crabbe's youth when she writes: "The world of Crabbe's youth, lacking in the elements of moral as of material beauty, made no such appeal to his imagination or affection and left him no such heritage of noble memories as inspired *The Cotter's Saturday Night* and the incomparable portrait of the deep-natured James Carlyle."[15] The violence of the elder Crabbe's character was not to come to the fore for another ten years or so. At the time of which we are speaking he seems to have been domestic and by no means inconsiderate of his family; if what has been almost universally assumed by critics to be a reference to him in the fifth of his son's *Tales,* "The Patron," may bear witness, he was respected by his son.

Of the poet himself, for the first seven years of his life, we know next to nothing—although what we can surmise is significant. All his biographers have attempted to reconstruct at least one incident in his earliest life from the fragment *Infancy* which was left among his papers at the time of his death, but there seems justifiable doubt as to the accuracy of the details the poet has recorded. This poem, and one posthumous tale, "Silford Hall," as well as various lines imbedded in his longer works, are only enough to indicate that he was an extraordinarily sensitive child, but whether the wistfulness which hangs about these two poems on childhood is an accurate representation of Crabbe's earliest state of mind is hard to know. It is likely that the psychological aura was at least as much invented by the old man for poetic effect as it was actually remembered.

The child was also bookish, which seems to have pleased the elder Crabbe, for he determined that his eldest son should have as many educational advantages as he could provide. At the age, probably, of about seven, the boy was sent to a school at "Bungay, on the borders of Norfolk, where it was hoped the activity

14 *Life,* p. 7.

15 L. J. Wylie, "The England of George Crabbe," *Social Studies in English Literature,* New York, 1916, p. 68.

of his mind would be disciplined into orderly diligence."[16] Except for one horrible anecdote in the *Life*[17] and possible references in *The Borough*, Letter XXIV, we know nothing of the child's years at this place.

According to the biographer: "When he was in his eleventh or twelfth year, it having now been determined that he should follow the profession of a surgeon, he was removed to a school of somewhat superior character, kept by Mr. Richard Haddon, a skillful mathematician, at Stowmarket, in the same county; and here, inheriting his father's talent and predilection for mathematical science, he made considerable progress in such pursuits."[18] It was, so far as we know, at Stowmarket that he made his first attempt at writing verse, "a stanza of doggerel, cautioning [a certain] little damsel against being too much elevated about a new set of blue ribands to her straw bonnet."[19] The child is father of the man. It was also at Stowmarket that he acquired the foundations of the fair classical education, pursued later without further academic prodding, which made it possible for him to be ordained when he came under the protection of Burke.

When he was fourteen, his formal education ended, and he was apprenticed, under indenture,[20] to a surgeon at Wickham-Brook, near Bury St. Edmunds. He was treated there as a farm-hand rather than as an apprentice, and, his father having been

---

[16] *Life*, p. 15. To what extent "The Patron," *Tales* V, 52–56, which expresses the sentiments of a borough-bailiff with a poetical son, is autobiographical it is impossible to say. It is certainly not beyond belief that Crabbe was drawing on memory when he had the father say:

> "The Boy," said he, "Will neither trade nor farm;
> He for both law and physic is unfit;
> Wit he may have, but cannot live on wit:
> Let him his talents then to learning give,
> Where verse is honour'd, and where poets live."

[17] *Life*, p. 16.   [18] *Ibid.*   [19] *Life*, pp. 16–17.

[20] Crabbe's third letter to Burke, or, as Huchon calls it from the fact that Burke sent it to Sir Charles Bunbury, who took a kindly interest in the poet, the "Bunbury Letter," printed as an appendix in *Life* and also in *Huchon*, p. 493. This letter was unknown to the Biographer, who states, p. 19, that there were no indentures.

made to see the injustice of this exploitation, he was removed from the situation and placed "with a Mr. Page, a surgeon at Woodbridge, a market town seventeen miles from Aldborough."[21] It is to be noticed that during these years he was never far from the vicinity of his native town, and it was no doubt during this period that he was receiving many of those impressions of the Suffolk port which were to find expression later in his verse.

Crabbe's apprenticeship at Woodbridge ended in 1775. From the time he left home in about 1761, he had been exposed to what must have been much the accepted life of the eighteenth-century schoolboy and apprentice. Of the exploitation by his first master at Wickham-Brook, he later wrote to Burke:

I rebelled in my servitude, for it became grievous. My Father was informed of his Son's idleness and disobedience; he came, and was severe in his correction of them: I knew myself then injur'd and became obstinate, and a second visit of my Father's put an end to my slavery; he took me home with him, and with me two-thirds of the money he had advanced.[22]

We can only speculate on the lonely agonies endured by the child rebelling, and knowing himself to be justly rebelling, against his determined elders; or upon his grateful elation when, after having been punished, he finally won his point. It is not easy for a child to rebel, and it is usually even more difficult for him to convince anyone that he is justified in his rebellion. The fact that the child Crabbe was finally successful may certainly have been a contributing factor in the formation of whatever Burke noticed as his "pure and worthy character," for something of essential rightness had been put to trial, and confirmed.

But these were not all years of unhappiness and rebellion. During his years at Stowmarket he acquired, or perhaps we should say sharpened, his first taste for learning, and at Woodbridge he had not only the fellowship of "companions suited to

21 *Life,* p. 19.

22 "Bunbury Letter," *Huchon,* p. 494.

his mind and habits,"[23] but he first loved the woman who was to become his wife. Here he met Miss Sarah Elmy, a young lady whose family, though at the time in reduced circumstances, still ranked as gentlefolk. She lived with her uncle, Mr. Tovell, at Parham, a few miles distant from Woodbridge, and is the "Mira" who appears in so many of Crabbe's juvenile verses, and is possibly to be identified with "Laura" of "The Lover's Journey" (*Tales* X), which we shall have occasion to discuss later. The fact that although four years older than he and of a higher station, she was nevertheless willing to accept seriously the addresses of a youth of eighteen indicates that Crabbe must already have begun to display something of the "mind and feelings of a gentleman" upon which Burke was later to remark to Reynolds.[24] Some indication of Crabbe's reaction to her favorable reception of him may be seen in a poem written at Aldborough two years later, when his situation was considerably less pleasant and he was undoubtedly looking backward with nostalgia. The peculiarly "un-romantic" juxtaposition of love and reason is particularly interesting:

> A wanton chaos in my breast raged high,
> A wanton transport darted in mine eye;
> False pleasure urged, and ev'ry eager care,
> That swell the soul to guilt and to despair.
> My Mira came! be ever blest the hour,
> That drew my thoughts half way from folly's power;
> She first my soul with loftier notions fired;
> I saw their truth, and as I saw admired;
> With greater force returning reason moved,
> And as returning reason urged, I loved;
> Till pain, reflection, hope, and love allied
> My bliss precarious to a surer guide— . . .

> [*Mira*, 1–12.]

It was also during these years at Woodbridge that he tasted the thrill of his first literary success, when he "had the misfor-

23 *Life*, p. 19.

24 *Life*, p. 90.

tune"[25] to gain the prize in a poetical competition conducted by Wheble's *Lady's Magazine*—a copy of which the biographer saw, but which seems since to have been quite lost[26]—with a poem on "Hope." The concluding lines are preserved in the *Life* and are worth repeating here as the earliest example of Crabbe's use of that verse form which was to become so peculiarly his own:

> But, above all, the POET owns thy powers—
> HOPE leads him on, and every fear devours;
> He writes, and, unsuccessful, writes again,
> Nor thinks the last laborious work in vain;
> New schemes he forms, and various plots he tries,
> To win the laurel, and possess the PRIZE.[27]

This fragment shows technical competence not above that which could be attained by almost anyone, and, it must be confessed, gives little indication of Crabbe's later power, but something of the quality of mind from which that later power was to spring does appear in *Inebriety, a Poem* which he somehow found means to publish at Ipswich in 1775, before he had left Woodbridge. I cannot agree with Saintsbury that *"Inebriety* and such other youthful things are not to be counted,"[28] for, although the poem abounds in technical inadequacies, it is original in choice of subject[29] and in treatment quite characteristic of its author. Had it been written six or seven years later, after Burke had given Crabbe some help with his numbers, it would hardly be a poem to be disregarded. For our purposes it is interesting because it leaves no doubt as to the attention with which Crabbe was studying Pope—a study which he acknowledges not

[25] George Crabbe [poet], "Biographical Account of the Rev. George Crabbe, L.L.B.," *The New Monthly Magazine,* vol. IV, no. 24 (Jan. 1, 1816), p. 512. The son makes reference to this in *Life,* p. 21.

[26] See the Prefaces to volumes I and II of the A. W. Ward edition of Crabbe's poems, vols. I–III, Cambridge, 1905–1907. All quotations from the poetry are taken from this edition, though I have conformed to the early editions in omitting the braces to indicate triplets.

[27] *Life,* p. 21; reprinted in Ward, vol. I, p. 4.

[28] "Crabbe," *Essays in English Literature, 1780–1860,* London, 1895, p. 15.

[29] This is also pointed out by Huchon, p. 58, who suggests that Crabbe might have intended this poem as the side of the picture not presented by Gay in *Wine.*

only by quoting in footnotes those passages from Pope's works which he directly imitates, but also in his amusing preface. We need notice now only that at this early date Crabbe made an explicit denial in *Inebriety* of the primitivistic attitude which he later attacked in *The Village,* and that it was in this 1775 publication that Crabbe presents the first of those pictures of humble life which were later to do much to make him famous. We may notice also that although as a *genre* the "Imitation" may have been somewhat old-fashioned in 1775, it had been hallowed by a good and still-living authority, and would not have been on the grounds that it was an "Imitation" disparaged for lack of "originality."

The relatively happy situation at Woodbridge did not continue long. If, as at least one critic would have had us believe,[30] the artistic success of creative writing depends upon a "traumatic experience" endured by the author in childhood or youth, we need not search further than the six years from the ending of his apprenticeship in 1775 to his meeting with Burke in 1781 for the explanation of Crabbe's power. We have for this period fairly detailed accounts in the *Life* and in Huchon's redaction, and I shall not recapitulate the biographer's narration of Crabbe's return to Aldborough to find his father a furied sot, or of the weary months during which he endured the indignity of working as a common laborer on Slaughden quay, the waterfront of Aldborough—a situation which in the class-conscious eighteenth century must indeed have seemed an indignity to the youth who had won a poetry prize and who had seen his long poem in print.[31] But most of all it seems to have been his father's drunkenness and lack of "oeconomy" that troubled him. Although I have no proof of the fact, I assume that it was as much of this period as to one later, when he was trying to establish himself as a surgeon in Aldborough, that Crabbe refers

[30] Edmund Wilson, *The Wound and the Bow,* New York, 1947.

[31] "He wrote upon every occasion, and without occasion . . . and began to think of succeeding in the highest line of composition, before he had made one good and commendable effort in the lowest." *Life,* p. 21, quoted from the 1816 "Biographical Account" by Crabbe himself, p. 512.

in one of the letters to Burke first published by Professor Wecter:

. . . my affection and my Duty to my father, leads me to avoid him. —My father and I are in perfect agreement; we parted with every appearance of it and I am persuaded there was Deceit in none; but if I live in the same Place I know that it is impossible to please him and others or myself . . . his employments, his inclinations, his connexions and mode of living are so different from my own that there is no way to preserve that Harmony there is and should be betwixt us, but by our Seperation [sic] . . .[32]

During a brief period of comparative good fortune, where he was employed as apothecary and surgeon by the parish, Crabbe was able to study and, apparently, to save a little money.[33] He read medical books in Latin, studied the *materia medica,* and devoted himself, to the total exclusion of any concern with poetry, entirely to that professional career, in which he was already beginning to feel ill at ease.[34]

In the autumn of 1776 Crabbe somehow got together enough money to enable him to spend a few months in London. He writes of this to Burke:

After one year, I left my little business to the care of a neighbouring surgeon, and came to London, where I attended the lectures of Messrs. Orme and Lowder on Midwifery, and occasionally stole round the hospitals to observe those remarkable cases which might indeed, but which probably never would, occur to me again. On my return I found my substitute had contracted a close intimacy with my rival. He cheated me and lost my business. The second woman who committed herself to my care, died before the month after her delivery was expired; and the more I became qualified for my profession, the less occasion I found for these qualifications. My business was trifling and lay amongst the poor. I had a sister who starved with me; and on her account it now pains me to say we often wanted bread; we were unwilling to add to my Father's distress by letting

32 Dixon Wecter, "Four Letters from Crabbe to Burke," *R.E.S.,* XIV (July, 1938), p. 303.

33 *Huchon,* p. 65, corrects the Biographer at this point.

34 *Ibid.*

him see ours, and we fasted with much fortitude. Every one knew me to be poor; I was dunned for the most trifling sums, and compelled to pay the rent of my hut weekly, for my landlord was Justice of the Corporation and a man of authority. My druggist, a good-natured Quaker, gave me some friendly hints. My friends and advisers who had been zealous for my fixing in this place, entirely deserted me for this reason only, that I had not been successful by following their advice. After three years spent in the misery of successless struggle, I found it necessary for me to depart, and I came to London.[35]

Of the disappointments, the hardships, the anguish of that second trip to London, at times so eloquently and always poignantly recorded in the "Poet's Journal"[36] and in the "Bunbury Letter," it would be a presumption to write here. The "Journal" is surely one of the most touching documents of the eighteenth century, and deserves to be read in its entirety, while the letter to Burke is no longer inaccessible. When we consider that in the case of the "Journal," written to be read by his loved "Mira," Crabbe was deliberately concealing the worst of his misfortunes, while in the letter he is obviously writing with the utmost restraint, we begin to imagine the quiet horror he endured for almost a year, until "he fixed, impelled by some propitious influence, in some happy moment, upon EDMUND BURKE, one of the first of Englishmen, and, in the capacity and energy of his mind, one of the greatest of human beings."[37]

3

Crabbe's early biography is of some importance because the evidence is so strong as to be conclusive that it was from the observations and experiences of these early years as seen and remembered through a miasma of humiliation and actual physical deprivation, that Crabbe drew the materials for his first three major works. In the *Tales* (1812) and *Tales of the Hall* (1819) the horizon is considerably widened, although in each

---

35 "Bunbury Letter," *Huchon*, p. 495.

36 *Life*, pp. 54–84.

37 *Life*, p. 86, from the "Biographical Account," p. 513.

case there are sections in which Aldborough is clearly recognizable; but when Crabbe came for the second time to London in 1780,[38] the metal for some of his finest poetry had already been tempered by hardship, and was only waiting to be sharpened and burnished by his experiences in the capital and by the drudgery of composition and correction. In the latter endeavor, at least, he found assistance; but he found assistance, it must be emphasized, not alone because he was able to write some promising verses, as deeply from certain conventions congenial to Burke as those verses were mined, but also because, to repeat again the words of his son, he had "exhibited the traits of a pure and worthy character." This it is important to recognize, because Crabbe is at bottom, as well as sometimes on the surface, a moral poet, and his morality was the product of the same tempering as his verse.

We can make no more than a sane guess as to what of Crabbe's work Burke saw, but it is not at all difficult to understand why he liked it. As the biographer stated, the poems gave evidence of genius, and Crabbe showed himself a man of character, and genius and character were two attributes which Burke was prepared to appreciate and reward. Some critics in discussing Crabbe and endeavoring to account for his success, have rather unkindly pointed out that the period from 1780 to 1800 was a low watermark in English poetry, and have assumed that "some readers may have had an uncomfortable though only half-conscious feeling that if they had not a poet in Crabbe they had not a poet at all. At all events they made up their minds that they had a poet in him."[39] This assumption, though convenient, seems to me unnecessary to explain Crabbe's initial success with *The Village* and his rise in fame after the 1807 edition of the *Poems* and the appearance of *The Borough* and the *Tales in Verse* at short intervals thereafter. The fact is that Crabbe's poems are such as would have struck any fancy schooled on, and appreciating, the satiric-didactic mode of so much

[38] The chronology hinted at in the "Bunbury Letter" would indicate it must have been in late June or July of 1780

[39] Saintsbury, *op. cit.*, p. 30.

eighteenth-century poetry. Whatever may have been his "native" genius, Crabbe was in one center of his age in respect to his taste.

The statement must read, "he was in *one* center of his age," for the period of the late eighteenth and early nineteenth centuries, like any other time, had several "centers"—was, in fact, so varied in its tastes that generalizations about it are apt to be catchwords rather than considered judgments. It is, however, with only one of those various tastes that we are concerned here —the great tradition extending from Dryden, through Pope, to Johnson.

Canon Ainger mentions in his study of Crabbe that at the time of its appearance it was generally assumed that *The Village* was a rejoinder to Goldsmith's *Deserted Village,* and the fact that Crabbe quotes a line from the latter poem, "passing rich on forty pounds a year," would seem to justify that impression.[40] Whatever Crabbe's immediate motives in composing his poem might have been—aside from the fact that he was understandably eager to make the most of Burke's patronage— it is clear from careful reading that its roots go below Goldsmith. The very opening lines point to where we may look for the genesis of the poem:

THE Village Life, and every care that reigns
O'er youth peasants and declining swains;
What labour yields, and what, that labour past,
Age, in its hour of languor, finds at last;
What form the real picture of the poor,
Demand a song—the Muse can give no more.
Fled are those times when, in harmonious strains,
The rustic poet praised his native plains.
No shepherds now, in smooth alternate verse,
Their country's beauty or their nymphs' rehearse;
Yet still for these we frame the tender strain,
Still in our lays fond Corydons complain,
And shepherds' boys their amorous pains reveal,
The only pains, alas! they never feel.

[*The Village,* 1–14.]

40 Alfred Ainger, *Crabbe* (English Men of Letters), New York, 1903, p. 48.

These lines are enough to indicate that Crabbe, like Johnson, whose opinions on the pastoral were by no means consistent but who in general disapproved of it, found that "its inherent improbability always forces dissatisfaction on the mind." Very likely he was first struck by this, as Ainger suggests, during his early life, when his father read aloud to the assembled family, for there can hardly be any doubt that some conventional Augustan pastorals found their way into an evening's recitation along with the graver works of Milton, Pope, and Young. If such were the case, he was struck by the improbability for the same reason that anyone is struck by an improbability in art, namely a failure of correspondence between the work of art and life. Crabbe, from his earliest years, lived in the midst of pastoral surroundings—the real pastoral surroundings—and with the literalness of a child was quick to observe that the murmurings of a spurned Corydon had little relevance to country life as it actually was. *The Deserted Village,* more than most "pastorals" of the time, did present a reality, whatever may have been the tone imparted to that reality by Goldsmith's own temperament, and it was, indeed, the very reality of the poem which commended it to John Scott of Amwell, a Quaker friend of Johnson's, who wrote of it:

This is not poetical fiction, but historical truth. We have here no imaginary Arcadia, but the real country; no poetical swains, but the men who actually drive the plough, or wield the scythe, the sickle, the hammer, or the hedging bill.

We must observe, however, that Scott adds:

But though nothing is invented, something is suppressed. The rustick's hour of relaxation is too rarely so innocent: it is too often contaminated with extravagance, anger, and profanity: describing vice and folly, however, will not prevent their existing; and it is agreeable to forget for a moment, the reality of their existence.[41]

Crabbe's objection to *The Deserted Village,* if he had any, might have been that though it is agreeable to forget, it is better to

[41] *Critical Essays on some of the Poems of Several English Poets,* London, 1785, p. 271.

remember; but he may also have recognized the idealization of Auburn in its happier days as having some justification in terms of the poem itself, for the fact seems to be that in *The Village* Crabbe was moved to the presentation of a level of truth somewhat different from that to which Goldsmith aspired: not the kind of truth presenting an ideal to serve as a basis of comparison with something else,[42] nor truth as a vehicle for moral animadversions, but a picture of actually existing circumstances which, in their own right, were worthy of presentation in order to dispel a falsehood.

We shall return to the falsehood in a moment; what we wish briefly to notice now is the relationship of the poem to the pastoral, which, as a form, had undergone radical changes through the eighteenth century. Mr. Varley H. Lang points out that if "the *Village* is not such a bolt from the blue as most literary historians would have us believe," it is because it "forms a link in a series of changes and additions in the Pastoral form," the progress of which he traces in his article.[43] Mr. Lang is undoubtedly correct in this assertion, and his illustrations, drawn from Allan Ramsay's *The Gentle Shepherd,* Swift's *Town Eclogue,* Jago's *The Scavengers,* and Churchill's *Prophecy of Famine* leave little doubt as to the intrusion of realistic "low" detail into the pastoral tradition, particularly in the form of the "Town Eclogue," usually a parody of the conventional eclogue dealing with town characters instead of those from the country

42 Bate uses the poems of Goldsmith as an example of "a romanticization of subject matter" which "long precedes the deliberate romanticization of the aesthetic medium." (Walter J. Bate, *From Classic to Romantic,* Cambridge, Mass., 1946, p. 168.) By "romanticization" I assume he refers to passages such as the opening lines, or lines 97–120 of *The Deserted Village,* where Goldsmith paints an idyllic view of the pre-depopulation village—a view which we have little reason to believe was ever literally true—in order to contrast it with the present unfortunate state of the community.

43 "Crabbe and the Eighteenth Century," *E.L.H.,* vol. V, no. 4 (Dec. 1938), pp. 305–333. We might note also, with Rose Marie Thale in "Crabbe's *Village* and Topographical Poetry" [*J.E.G.P.,* LV (Oct. 1956), pp. 618–623], that the form of the poem may be dictated in part by another literary convention. I think probably Miss Thale is correct when she suggests that the conventions of the "topographical poem" influenced *The Village,* but, as is evident, I do not agree with her as to the "seeming formlessness of the work, its odd combination of discordant elements."

and substituting, for example, piles of manure and gutters for the hills and rivulets of its model. That Crabbe knew many of these "Town Eclogues" cannot be doubted; that he knew Churchill's poetry is certain, since he quotes *The Author* twice in mottoes for Letter III of *The Borough*.

This provides some trace of a literary stream into which Crabbe poured his own creative impulses, and as far as it goes, the relationship established between *The Village* and the eighteenth-century "realistic pastoral" is a perfectly valid one; but the sources of Crabbe's poetic power are more positively a part of the eighteenth century than this negative concern with one aspect of the period would indicate. Crabbe's genius springs not from mere protest against a literary convention, but from an outlook toward life which throughout his poetic career retained his allegiance, which underlies the immediate fabric of all his poetry. This view was given artistic expression very early in English neo-classicism, and underlies Pope's famous remark that to know mankind we should study men. The statement about the "proper study" covered only part of it, however; for there may clearly be many ways of studying men, and it is the way men are studied which distinguishes neo-classic poetry of the eighteenth century from the poetry, for example, of Wordsworth, who was also devoted to the study of men but who is scarcely neo-classic.

If we look at the productions of those men who are properly ignored by the "romantic hunters" and exclude those of such entirely eighteenth-century figures as Thomson, Smart, Chatterton, Collins, and Gray, we can establish what I shall call one tradition in the poetry of the eighteenth century. Those major figures with whom, after our historical surgery, we shall be concerned are Dryden, Pope, Swift, and Johnson. There are other authors who were important and who at the time were influential and highly esteemed—Addison, for example, and Young in his satires—and we shall have occasion to look at Gay and Prior, but it scarcely needs to be pointed out that in the judgment of their own time and in the judgment of most critics until well into the nineteenth century, these four men (with only the possible exception of Swift) were classics, and the ways in which they handled the modes they had essayed, established precedents from which only the more daring poets cared to depart, in serious productions at least, until well after Wordsworth published his famous manifesto.

What held these men together was not a matter of technique, though that helped, and though the heroic couplet became the badge of most of their works in verse, for the technique itself was only a manifestation of their deeper concern with form, which in turn was a result of their effort to achieve a timeless objectivity which could only be lost by outward eccentricity. Nor were they united merely through chance "influences," for the influence of one generation upon the next over a period of more than a century is by no means determined—Smart and Collins could hardly have avoided reading Dryden and Pope, yet they are not in the current with which we are concerning ourselves. What makes it possible for us to trace a tradition at all was a view of life and art which these men shared. I could term this view "neo-classic," except that the word has connotations which would tend to exclude Crabbe from the discussion. Crabbe was never "neo-classic" in the sense applicable to the four giants; he was never concerned with the principles of classical art and never consciously attempted to emulate those principles. But there is an outlook upon life which he shares with his predecessors in this particular tradition. It may be disquieting to some, since the term seems under a shadow of critical opprobrium, that I call that outlook "realistic."

The use of the word in the present context has some precedent in criticism, and seems inevitably to arise whenever Crabbe is discussed. Crabbe's writing has, of course, almost innumerable points of contact with the writings of the earlier eighteenth century; since these contacts are so nearly innumerable, I hope, by focusing my attention on this very inclusive one, to avoid the folly of attempting to number them. I intend to signify more by the word "realism" than merely the use of dirty linen as an item in poetic description as opposed to the use of clean linen, no linen at all, or supernal linen. Nor do I necessarily intend that the word is to be taken as the diametrical opposite of "romantic," for romantic literature must have some contact somewhere with what the poet has experienced as a part of the real world of observation and sensation. In the case of such poets as the prophetic Blake the relationship may appear exceedingly tenuous, but it is there, only obscured by the poet's own personality or prejudices. Here we begin to see the root of a definition, for Blake's observation of the external world seems to have become more and more "private" as he grew older and met continual rebuffs, and this "private" observation was something our realistic quadrumvirate would neither have understood nor approved of. For them the real world was the place of their abode, a place which was rife with imperfections, but which they did not for that reason turn their backs upon. They were reconciled to living in it, and were eager to improve, even to explain it, but it was for them "not a point of departure, but the place where they made their home."[44] Their suggested improvements and their explanations were invariably based upon what they knew to be fact and, what is more important, upon what every man in his right mind knew to be fact. Although they might not all accept the resigned pessimism of "whatever is, is right," they were at least concerned with looking at "whatever is," and with looking at it clearly and without odd interpretations. They were fascinated by the surrounding scene and by their own times and the people who made those times great or disgraceful as the case might be. Such an objective interest working itself out creatively sometimes by attraction, sometimes by revulsion, is the essential spirit of what I hope to convey by "realism."

A concern such as this with one's own times, to be sure, is by no means peculiar to the neo-classic temperament. It is, rather, the particular manifestation of this interest in certain authors which makes it proper for us to term them realists. There is, in realistic art, no "transformation," no losing sight of what ob-

44 Arthur McDowall, *Realism: A Study in Art and Thought,* London, 1918, p. 4. The statement quoted is applicable to the group I am discussing even though McDowall did not so apply it.

jects really are in the sight of sensible men, and our realistic authors, having the keen desire to correct the imperfections which they no less than a "romantic" see around them, keep their poetry firmly attached to their observations. Whether Dryden discusses the court of Israel's monarch or Johnson the conquests of Swedish Charles, the world they show is recognizable, intelligible, and concrete. It is a world we can deal with practically, and presented not as the poets might wish it to be, but as they saw it.

When, as they frequently did, they saw bad things in the world, their art, expressing, condemning, correcting these things, turned, as naturally as a daisy turns toward the sun, in the direction of satire. Satire is one of the ways in which art works itself out by revulsion from the observed world. It may take a great many forms, all of which we need not discuss, but all these forms have this in common: they are reflecting observed reality, whether by ludicrous distortion of reality as in *The Dunciad,* or admonition on the basis of reality as in the last part of *The Vanity of Human Wishes;* whether they are personal or social, kindly or vindictive; whether their object is exploded to enormity, as in *MacFlecknoe,* or reduced to absurd insignificance, as in the portrait of Sporus, there is an objectivity which makes the satire comprehensible to anyone who can observe the reality upon which it is based.

Johnson, in his dictionary, defined satire as "A poem in which wickedness or folly is censured," and went on to point out that "proper *satire* is distinguished, by the generality of the reflections, from a *lampoon,* which is aimed against a particular person." In his definition of "lampoon" he calls it ". . . censure written not to reform, but to vex." This leads us to another, and very important, thing which all forms of satire, at least as conceived by the eighteenth century, have in common: that is, there is implied by the censure of wickedness or folly a desire to work some change for the better in the reality which the poems reflect. The most obvious change Pope seems endeavoring to bring about in *The Dunciad* is in the temper of his enemies, which is pleasant for him but not necessarily a benefit to the world at large. In this poem, however, though it verges at points on the lampoon, it is clear that there is a much larger and more profound purpose in view: to eliminate the stultifying, and genuine, "dulness" from the world of letters. This desire may lead Pope into perversities and at times into mere petulant lampooning, but it remains nevertheless the animating force of the poem however much the author's personal feuds may intrude themselves. Similarly, *The Vanity of Human Wishes* conforms to what we may call our rule, because there Johnson is trying to instruct, to *re-form* men in the fortitude necessary to meet the difficulties and the inevitable tragedy of humanity doomed to ultimate failure in its highest aspirations.

It is Johnson's two essays in the form which lead us to reject, for our purposes, an attribute commonly accorded satire: that is, all satire is not necessarily humorous. Not many readers laugh as they lay aside a copy of one of Johnson's satires, yet these poems, as all satires do, exhibit a radical concern with that incongruity between aspiration and achievement, between appearance and reality, which is the ultimate resource of humor.

Johnson's own definition applies most accurately to the Juvenalian satire which Dryden set up as a model, and his practice, as we know, conformed to this in his two imitations of Juvenal. But the satire of most of the eighteenth century, following Pope, tended toward the "comical" satire as Dryden called it, descending to the use of "miserable clenches" and condoning, if not actually sanctioning, the lampoon. The fact that he never lampoons is one of the things which distinguishes Crabbe's from the work of most of his fellow satirists, for he is above all a realist; he had a facility which he never lost, for seeing both sides of a question, and such an ability makes a sincere man slow to ridicule. Thus he put into practice the ideal of satire which for many of the eighteenth-century satirists remains little more than abstract precept. That Crabbe understood the nature of satire is not to be doubted by anyone who has read *The Village,* and the impression may be confirmed by the concluding lines of *The Borough:*

Man's vice and crime I combat as I can,
But to his GOD and conscience leave the man;
I search (a [Quixote!]) all the land about,
To find its giants and enchanters out,
(The giant-folly, the enchanter-vice,
Whom doubtless I shall vanquish in a trice;)
But is there man whom I would injure?—no!
I am to him a fellow, not a foe—
A fellow-sinner, who must rather dread
The bolt, then hurl it at another's head.
    No! let the guiltless, if there such be found,
Launch forth the spear, and deal the deadly wound;
How can I so the cause of virtue aid,
Who am myself attainted and afraid?
Yet, as I can, I point the powers of rhyme,
And, sparing criminals, attack the crime.

[*The Borough*, XXIV, 450–465.]

In another place (lines 29–30 of *The Borough*, VI) he remarks:

Beside, a Muse like mine, to satire prone,
Would fail in themes where there is praise alone.

Exactly. His muse was to satire prone, and his work is principally directed to combating the follies and crimes of men.[45] It is not the form of *The Village* which is important, even though its significance as demonstrating the difficulty with which Crabbe tore himself away from some of the more formal attributes of eighteenth-century verse cannot be doubted; it is the informing spirit behind the poem which gives it not only its great power but also its importance to a student of Crabbe.

[45] We may assume that this was his pastoral work too, although he writes to Elizabeth Charter, Nov. 11, 1815 (considerably after the writing of *The Village*, of course). "I know that you and 1 or 2 other obliging and serious Friends may, and probably will observe, that the Duties I complain of ought to be pleasant and to be very frank, this is my Vexation, that they are not. I have read of good and pious Priests, who have made it their 'Meat and drink,' their Joy and Delight, to be engaged with all their Hearts and Minds in these occupations, but I am not, and I am convinced that instructing Ignorance and correcting Vice are not my Talents, at least they do not suit my Turn of Mind and Temper. God forgive me! I am disgusted where I should pity and want to run away from the Object who expects from me Consolation and Sympathy." Broadley and Jerrold, p. 110.

4

In the following discussion of *The Village* we shall shortly turn to its position as a work in the tradition of realistic satire. In order, however, further to clarify its relationship to the tradition, we must examine in their historical relationships certain of the techniques which Crabbe employed, and continued to employ through a large part of his career.

It is interesting that all these techniques were available to him at the time he wrote. Crabbe was an innovator only in so far as he turned them to uses for which there was little or no precedent in the eighteenth century. His use of realistic detail in the representation of the more sordid and unpleasant aspects of rural life is most frequently pointed out as one of his original contributions to English poetry, but we have already noticed that he was able to draw on the "town eclogue" which incorporated such "low" details—details, that is, which were considered too commonplace or too disgusting properly to be admitted into the higher poetry—and the use of homely realism was by no means confined to that form; as a matter of fact, it had never been absent from English verse. In the immediate tradition with which we are concerned, however, its use had been confined almost entirely to light verse. Pope's imitation of Spenser, *The Alley,* comes immediately to mind as an example, but Pope himself had precedent for the use of "low" details, to name only one instance of many, in Ben Jonson's remarkable Epigram, "On the Famous Voyage":

> In the first jaws appear'd the ugly monster,
> Ycleped mud, which, when their oars did once stir,
> Belch'd forth an air as hot, as at the muster
> Of all your night-tubs, when the carts do cluster,
> Who shall discharge first his merd-urinous load:
> Through her womb they make their famous road . . .[46]

Gay's *Trivia* follows Jonson at a distance; Gay is much less coarse, much less ill-humored, and, indeed, less detailed than

---

[46] Ben Jonson, *Works,* 1875, vol. VIII, p. 235.

Jonson, but the poem has passages which are pertinent to our interest:

> When dirty waters from balconies drop
> And dext'rous damsels twirl the sprinkling mop,
> And cleanse the spatter'd sash, and scrub the stairs;
> Know Saturday's conclusive morn appears.
>
> [*Trivia*, Book II, 421–425.]

It is Swift who probably approaches more nearly to Crabbe than any other author of the eighteenth century not only in his sustained use of details in his poetry, but also in what Mr. Ricardo Quintana calls his "passion for seeing and for making the whole world see with eyes undimmed by folly and sentiment."[47] He even seems to use "low" detail with some social force not dissimilar to Crabbe's own in his *A Description of a City Shower,* a poem which has been frequently alluded to and quoted in connection with Crabbe, and his *A Description of the Morning* is also remarkable for accuracy of observation and delineation. Even more interesting is *Baucis and Philemon,* where we find the combination of humble personages, narrative, and specific detail:

> . . . And then the hospitable sire
> Bid Goody Baucis mend the fire;
> While he from out the chimney took
> A flitch of bacon off the hook,
> And freely from the fattest side
> Cut out large slices to be fried . . .[48]

The association of "low" details with narrative verse, the medium in which Crabbe was principally to employ them later, was well established long before the appearance of his earliest poems. As we shall notice in a later essay, Prior had written little fabliaux similar to Swift's, and scarcely a miscellany appeared that did not contain several of them. It must be pointed out, however, that before Crabbe's time "low" detail does not

47 *The Mind and Art of Jonathan Swift,* Oxford, 1936, p. 65.

48 Swift, *Works,* New York, 1859, vol. I, p. 239.

seem to have been put to much use in poetry of a serious tone
except in such isolated passages as we shall presently observe in
Pope. The only possible exception to this is the poetry of "honest Duck," Stephen Duck, the thresher-poet, and even he seems
to have made only one excursion into this kind of writing before
he turned his full attention to the flattery of the Queen in
innocuous odes and pastorals.

It must be admitted that the thresher-poet was considered
more as a curiosity than as a man of letters, but just as Duck
does not seem particularly to have shocked anybody in the early
century with *The Thresher's Labour,* the poem which Crabbe
had in mind when he wrote, so I do not believe we need to
assume that *The Village,* upon its appearance, occasioned either
surprise or indignation. After all, Dr. Johnson himself had referred to it as "original, vigorous, and elegant,"[49] and this was
quite in accord with his expressed preference for the *domestica
facta* as materials for literature. In this Johnson was by no
means alone. Joseph Warton, in his *Essay on the Genius and
Writings of Pope,* had written:

> In truth the *Domestica Facta* are more interesting, as well as more
> useful: more interesting, because we all think ourselves concerned in
> the actions and fates of our countrymen; more useful, because the
> characters and manners bid the fairest to be true and natural, when
> they are drawn from models with which we are exactly acquainted.[50]

Warton was at this point speaking of drama; the *domestica
facta* to which he refers are by no means the poor-houses of
Aldborough. The emphasis on "true and natural" manners,
however, and the fact that these are to be drawn from models
with which we are acquainted is interesting even though the
context does not allow us to apply the quotation to any poetry
such as Crabbe might have written. But Warton makes some

[49] In a letter written to Sir Joshua Reynolds, who had induced Johnson to read
the poem and offer minor corrections. On the extent of the corrections, see Boswell's *Life of Samuel Johnson* (ed. G. B. Hill), Oxford, 1891, vol. IV, p. 202.
Crabbe rather apologetically included the letter in the preface to his poems of
1807. See Ward, vol I, p. 92.

[50] 4th edition, 1782, vol. I, p. 287.

remarks directly applicable to such poetry when, later in the
work, he quotes two passages from Pope's *Moral Essays:*

> Like some lone Chartreux stands the good old Hall,
> Silence without, and Fasts within the wall;
> No rafter'd roofs with dance and tabor sound,
> No Noontide-bell invites the country round;
> Tenants with sighs the smokeless tow'rs survey,
> And turn th'unwilling steeds another way;
> Benighted wanderers, the forest o'er
> Curse the sav'd candle, and unop'ning door;
> While the gaunt mastiff growling at the gate,
> Affrights the beggar whom he longs to eat.
>
> [Epistle III, 187–196.]

and:

> In the worst inn's worst room with mat half-hung,
> The floors of plaister, and the walls of dung,
> On once a flock-bed, but repair'd with straw,
> With tape-ty'd curtains, never meant to draw
> The George and Garter dangling from that bed,
> Where tawdry yellow strove with dirty red,
> Great Villiers lies—alas! how chang'd from him,
> That life of pleasure and that soul of whim!
>
> [Epistle III, 299–306.]

Of these Warton remarks:

The use, the force, and the excellence of language certainly consists
in raising, *clear, complete* and *circumstantial* images, and in turning
readers into *spectators*. I have quoted the two preceding passages as
eminent examples of this excellence, of all others the most essential
in poetry. Every epithet here used, *paints* its object, and *paints* it
distinctly.

He goes on to make a plea for the . . .

. . . effect that the use of common and familiar words and objects,
judiciously managed, produces in poetry. . . A fastidious delicacy,
and a false refinement, in order to avoid meanness, have deterred
our writers from the introduction of such words; but DRYDEN

often hazarded it, and gave by it a secret charm, and a natural air to his verses. . .[51]

John Scott of Amwell, in the essay previously quoted, remarks that Milton "only mentions sound in general, but our Author [Goldsmith] descends to particulars, and those particulars are most happily selected . . ."[52]

It would not profit us to labor any further the point that many of Crabbe's contemporaries must have been quite prepared to witness a poet strike out on the paths which Crabbe selected. Those paths were new only in that never before had the "low" details been used to sustain a long poem of serious intent.

The use of the word "sustain" is not precise. None of Crabbe's poems, not even sections of *The Borough* such as "The Poor and their Dwellings" or "Abel Keene" or "Peter Grimes," is merely a tissue of low detail, and proportionally *The Village* has very considerably less than these. There can be no doubt, however, that the tone of *The Village* is somber—Crabbe's humor, so marked a feature of his later work, is here kept tightly leashed—and that this tone results from the almost overwhelming impression of the miseries and degradation of the poor with which we leave the poem, even though that impression is somewhat diminished in force, and designedly so diminished, by the concluding panegyric to Lord Robert Manners. The tone is also the result of description not involving the use of "low" details at all—descriptions as realistic and gloomy as the famous one of the heath in lines 63–78 of Book I could have found a place in almost any neo-classic verse; it is at least in part the effect of the straightforward presentation of some of the more disheartening activities of the villagers; of solemn exhortation by the poet; and of the one, slightly sentimental, soliloquy delivered by the

> Hoary swain, whose age
> Can with no cares except his own engage.

51 *Ibid.*, pp. 165–175.

52 John Scott of Amwell, *Critical Essays* . . . , p. 262.

In such a passage as the following:

> Here, wand'ring long amid these frowning fields,
> I sought the simple life that Nature yields;
> Rapine and Wrong and Fear usurp'd her place,
> And a bold, artful, surly, savage race;
> Who, only skill'd to take the finny tribe,
> The yearly dinner, or septennial bribe,
> Wait on the shore, and, as the waves run high,
> On the tost vessel bend their eager eye,
> Which to their coast directs its vent'rous way;
> [Their], or the ocean's miserable prey.
>
> > [*The Village,* I, 109–118.]

Whatever the tone here may be, it would be impossible to point out where "low" details intrude into the purest eighteenth-century diction. It is, indeed, not until we come to the description of the poorhouse that we find Crabbe presenting the first, except for a passage in *Inebriety,* and one of the greatest of his "Dutch paintings," a picture of poverty delineated with such memorable power that Jeffrey remarks:

We have known more than one of our unpoetical acquaintances, who declared they could never pass by a parish workhouse, without thinking of the description of it they had read at school in the Poetical Extracts.[53]

The passage must be quoted at length:

> Theirs is yon house that holds the parish poor,
> Whose walls of mud scarce bear the broken door;
> There, where the putrid vapours, flagging, play,
> And the dull wheel hums doleful through the day—
> There children dwell, who know no parents' care;
> Parents, who know no children's love, dwell there!
> Heart-broken matrons on their joyless bed,
> Forsaken wives, and mothers never wed;
> Dejected widows with unheeded tears,
> And crippled age with more than childhood fears;

---

[53] Francis Jeffrey, *Contributions to the Edinburgh Review*, London, 1846, vol. II, p. 275. The original review was of Crabbe's 1807 volume, and appeared in the *Edinburgh* in April, 1808.

The lame, the blind, and, far the happiest they!
The moping idiot and the madman gay.
Here too the sick their final doom receive,
Here brought, amid the scenes of grief, to grieve,
Where the loud groans from some sad chamber flow,
Mix'd with the clamours of the crowd below;

. . . .

Such is that room which one rude beam divides,
And naked rafters form the sloping sides;
Where the vile bands that bind the thatch are seen,
And lath and mud are all that lie between,
Save one dull pane, that, coarsely patch'd gives way
To the rude tempest, yet excludes the day.
Here, on a matted flock, with dust o'erspread,
The drooping wretch reclines his languid head;
For him no hand the cordial cup applies,
Or wipes the tear that stagnates in his eyes;
No friends with soft discourse his pain beguile,
Or promise hope till sickness wears a smile.

[*The Village* I, 228–241; 262–273.]

Now these lines are almost the only examples of "low" detail in the poem (in Book II the only lines which might be considered are those few describing the Sunday brawl, less than ten in all), and if we look at these closely we will be surprised to see how little detail there actually is. So far as the number of lines is concerned, the proportion of these lines to the whole of the poem is almost exactly the same as that of the lines quoted from Pope's *Third Moral Epistle* to that poem as a whole,[54] and they are no more imbued than those with descriptive matter. We have a house and the parish poor—by no means specific terms—then walls of mud, a broken door, putrid vapors, and a dull wheel. There is no more specific description until we

---

[54] There are other interesting parallels and differences between the passages. Pope and Crabbe use almost exactly the same number of nouns per line, while Crabbe uses verbs slightly more frequently, and adjectives markedly so. The figures with the average usages per line are:

	Nouns	Verbs	Adjectives
Pope	2.2	.88	.81
Crabbe	2.1	.93	1.2

reach the rude beam dividing the room with naked rafters and sloping sides. (The lines omitted between lines 243 and 262 contain the idea that the poor here consider the "cold charities of man to man"; an admonition by the poet leads into the second part of the quotation.) Here follow five lines of detailed description which lay the scene for the drooping wretch, who gives occasion for no details conceivably to be called "low." In other words, in all of the first book, there are not many more than thirteen lines which actually present "low" detail, and in the second book there are only about a half-dozen.

The tone of *The Village* is, in any case, by no means entirely the product of its detailed description of matters ordinarily excluded from polite poetry. I suggest that this tone does result, in part, from the blighted natural setting which Crabbe uses as his backdrop, but it results more forcefully from the uncompromising attitude of Crabbe toward his subject. The subject of the poem—"to paint the Cot / As Truth will paint it, and as Bards will not"—is not a cheerful one, and that fact in itself contributes initially to our impression of the poem, but Crabbe has not engaged to make it appear more cheerful than it is. He sees the village exactly as it is, and, as it is, it is worth recording in poetry. From that record, since "vice and misery demand the song," he points out how often the misery is the result of the vice, and implies that the vice itself may possibly arise from conditions beyond the control of any man:

> But these are scenes where Nature's niggard hand
> Gave a spare portion to the famish'd land;
> Hers is the fault, if here mankind complain
> Of fruitless toil and labour spent in vain.
>
> [*The Village* I, 131–134.]

This is not throwing the burden off on "nature," as it might appear had the idea been much emphasized in the course of the poem; it is not in any way to relieve men of moral responsibility; it is simply an example of Crabbe's fair and balanced presentation of the subject he chose, and of his adherence to the rarely-followed ideal of classical satire.

Mr. Strang would have us believe that Crabbe is a proper satirist only in those poems written before that long interval of twenty years which separates his earlier from his later work.[55] In a strictly formal sense of the word "satire" this may be true, and any attempt to advance him as a writer with none but satiric predispositions would be clearly foredoomed to failure should anyone want to make such an attempt; but the fact is that at almost no time does Crabbe depart from the precepts upon which satire is founded. It would, indeed, be difficult to say that his "satiric muse" ever deserted him, at least in those poems he himself chose to publish, although his satire became mellow and even gentle toward the end of his career, tending to the notice more of the minor foibles than of the great vices of men.[56] Like Dryden, he hopes "with Origen, that the Devil himself may at last be saved," and perhaps for that very reason he does not feel it appropriate to become splenetic.

Now there is just a little spleen in *The Village;* it is not a kindly poem. It seems reasonable to term it a satire in the same sense that *The Vanity of Human Wishes* is a satire, though it is not so evenly sustained as the greater poem; but the label is not to be insisted upon. To whatever genre the poem may belong, if it belongs to any, there can be no doubt that it belongs to the "realistic" tradition of the neo-classic giants. There is in this case not even a chronological discrepancy, for the poem received the correction and approbation of Ursa Major himself. It is not difficult to see why he approved. When Boswell writes, "Its sentiments as to the false notions of rustick happiness and rustick virtue, were quite congenial with his own,"[57] we can remember Johnson's characteristic determination to face up to reality; that characteristic in itself would have tended to make Johnson approve of Crabbe's poem.

---

[55] William Strang, *George Crabbe,* The Quain Essay for 1913, London, University of London Press, 1913, p. 30.

[56] *E.g., Posthumous Tales* II, 53–60. This "warm" satire seems, however, to be relatively lacking in the *New Poems by George Crabbe* [ed. Arthur Pollard], Liverpool University Press, 1960.

[57] *Life of Samuel Johnson,* edition cited, p. 202.

The Village, therefore, in the immediate tradition of the pastoral simply by force of its powerful repudiation of that tradition, is even more clearly in the tradition of eighteenth century realism. In fact, though the running battle between the two traditions had been almost definitely decided in favor of the latter by the weight of Dr. Johnson's opinion,[58] *The Village* was the great poetic expression of the victory, couched in the formal satiric mold which the eighteenth century accepted as one of the media for realistic expression. The fact that *The Village* is the only one of Crabbe's formal satires—all his early poems except for a few lyrics are in this form—which is a sustained success does in itself point to the limitations of his dependence upon the form: it was not form, but matter which primarily dictated the success of his writing.

Now accepting the fact that *The Village* is an inheritor of the realistic-satiric tradition, it is not easy to see at first glance just what vices and follies Crabbe is concerned with in the poem, for on one reading it gives the impression of a curious refusal to take sides on any issue except that of the formal pastoral itself. Obviously a poem of some 550 lines cannot be sustained on that issue alone, nor does Crabbe make an effort to do so. Probably the clearest explanation of exactly what he had in mind is a passage in Letter IX of *The Borough:*

> Along the wall, returning from the town,
> The weary rustic homeward wanders down;
> Who stops and gazes at such joyous crew,
> And feels his envy rising at the view;
> He the light speech and laugh indignant hears,
> And feels more press'd by want, more vex'd by fears.
> Ah! go in peace, good fellow, to thine home,
> Nor fancy these escape the general doom;
> Gay as they seem, be sure with them are hearts
> With sorrow tried; there's sadness in their parts.
> If thou couldst see them when they think alone,
> Mirth, music, friends, and these amusements gone;

58 H. E. Mantz, "Non-Dramatic Pastoral in Europe in the Eighteenth Century," *PMLA,* XXXI (1916), p. 443.

Couldst thou discover every secret ill
That pains their spirit, or resists their will;
Couldst thou behold forsaken Love's distress,
Or envy's pang at glory and success,
Or Beauty, conscious of the spoils of Time,
Or Guilt, alarm'd when Memory shows the crime—
All that gives sorrow, terror, grief, and gloom:
Content would cheer thee, trudging to thine home.
   There are, 'tis true, who lay their cares aside,
And bid some hours in calm enjoyment glide;
Perchance some fair-one to the sober night
Adds (by the sweetness of her song) delight;
And, as the music on the water floats,
Some bolder shore returns the soften'd notes;
Then, youth, beware, for all around conspire
To banish caution and to wake desire;
The day's amusement, feasting beauty, wine,
These accents sweet and this soft hour combine,
When most unguarded, then to win that heart of thine:
But see, they land! the fond enchantment flies,
And in its place life's common views arise.

[*The Borough* IX, 173–205.]

With this passage in mind, there is no need to see, as some have done, a lack of unity in *The Village,* nor need we say, as does Huchon, that "the chaplain has spoilt the poet,"[59] for the compliment to Lord Robert Manners at the end of the poem is entirely pertinent to the second of the "two idols to be smashed,"[60] as Strang calls the popular falsehoods which Crabbe is in this poem doing his utmost to dispel: the supposition on the part of the wealthy that the poor are somehow virtuous and happy, and the equally fallacious and somewhat pathetic assumption by the impoverished that their superiors in wealth and power are universally blessed with happiness and good fortune. It goes without saying that the viewpoint is not uniquely Crabbe's. So far as it applies to virtue, we may find somewhat the same sentiments in *The Essay on Man* (Epistle

---

[59] *Huchon,* p. 167.   [60] Strang, *Crabbe,* p. 36.

II, 231–234), and we need only to be reminded of Johnson's review of Soame Jenyns' *Free Enquiry into the Nature and Origin of Evil* to be aware that the sentimental conception of the blessings of poverty had been under attack long before the publication of Crabbe's poem. That it was the sentimental conception which Crabbe also attacked there can be no doubt, even if we assume so merely on the basis of the number of lines to which he assigns the task of showing the true state of the poor, their physical and moral depravity and their pathos (for Crabbe is by no means averse to pulling a pathetic string when the occasion invites). But this is not the whole picture. With the balanced viewpoint of the true satirist, Crabbe must show the other side of the coin. He must

> . . . show the great, those mightier sons of pride,
> How near in vice the lowest are allied. . .
>
> [*The Village* II, 89–90.]

while at the same time exhorting the poor, telling those:

> . . . ye poor, who still lament your fate,
> Forbear to envy those you call the great;
> And know, amid those blessings they possess,
> They are, like you, the victims of distress.
>
> [*The Village* II, 101–104.]

In *The Library* he had written:

> Some drops of comfort on the favour'd fall,
> But showers of sorrow are the lot of *all*,
>
> [*The Library*, 513–514.]

and this is the organizing theme of his later poem, a theme which he illustrates first by pointing out to the fortunate the misfortunes and little pleasures[61] of the poor, then by telling the poor themselves:

> Oh! if in life one noble chief appears,
> Great in his name, while blooming in his years;

[61] The opening passage of Book II of *The Village* is too often overlooked, overshadowed as it is by the sheer bulk of the unhappiness in Book I.

> Born to enjoy whate'er delights mankind,
> And yet to all you feel or fear resign'd;
> Who gave up joys and hopes, to you unknown,
> For pains and dangers greater than your own:
> If such there be, then let your murmurs cease,
> Think, think of him, and take your lot in peace.
> And such there was:—Oh! grief, that checks our pride!
> Weeping we say, there was—for Manners died. . .
>
> [*The Village* II, 107–116.]

He rounds off the whole by addressing both parties:

> Cease then that grief and let those tears subside;
> If Passion rule us, be that passion pride;
> If Reason, Reason bids us strive to raise
> Our fallen hearts, and be like him we praise.
>
> [*The Village* II, 183–186.]

This is no sentimental exhortation to find comfort, and had Crabbe a further comment to make, he might well have appended to this passage the note which he actually attached to the line, "Content would cheer thee trudging to thine home," in the passage just quoted from *The Borough:* "This is not offered as a reasonable source of contentment, but as one motive for resignation: there would not be so much envy if there were more discernment." Crabbe knew perfectly well that the rich have chances for happiness which they perhaps neglect, but this only in a very small degree can mitigate geniune misfortune which they share with all humanity; at the same time he knew that the poor are sometimes unnecessarily unhappy.[62] The formal balance between rich and poor expounded in the poem is clearly in direct contact with the classical conception of satire, and with the ideal of satire as expounded by Dryden in his famous essay. The "lesson" which he had in mind is

---

[62] See *Tales of the Hall* XI, 391 ff. Even though we must remember that this passage was much later than *The Village*, it is an appropriate reminder that Crabbe, at least in his later years, came to see certain virtues in humble life. The idea is so little developed, however, that it would be unfair to accuse Crabbe of succumbing, in his good fortune, to ideas which he had condemned in his bad.

essentially the classical one of resignation, a theme which runs throughout the body of his works.[63]

The "lesson," however, has by some critics been lost sight of in the details of the poem, so the common reader may be excused if he fails to keep it clearly in view. I mentioned before that there is spleen in *The Village,* and as a matter of fact the protest against sentimentalism never quite worked itself out in Crabbe. We find it even in some of the *Posthumous Tales,* and in all of his works on parochial themes it plays a major part in setting the tone and establishing the point of view for the reader. Canon Ainger states that it was the starting point of his desire to portray village life truly,[64] and this may well have been true; it may even be true, as McDowall contends, that "realism usually grows grim by reaction against a sentimental view of things, and this is illustrated in Crabbe's case; he intentionally darkened his *Village* to counteract Goldsmith's rosy tints."[65] Whether he intentionally darkened the picture in reaction against the sentimental view of rural life I suppose there is no way to determine today. Huchon remarks, "Alas! I much fear that the gloomier picture is also the truer one,"[66] and it is convenient for us to agree with this, for from our standpoint it does not much matter whether Crabbe was spreading his darker hues with undue generosity or not. The thing that interests us is that he did paint darkly, more darkly than any other modern poet writing in English before his time.[67] Goldsmith, after all,

[63] See, for example, Book IV of *Tales of the Hall,* the opening of which, to line 130, is beautifully suffused with this idea without ever leading to an explicit statement.

[64] Ainger, *Crabbe,* p. 300.

[65] McDowall, *Realism,* p. 67.   [66] *Huchon,* p. 170.

[67] Mr. Franklin P. Batdorf has maintained in *N. & Q.* vol. CXCIV no. 22 (29 Oct. 1949), pp. 477–478 that Crabbe's attitude toward his subject was anticipated by almost a year in four lines from Cowper's *Hope* (lines 7–10):

"The poor, inur'd to drudg'ry and distress,
Act without aim, think little, and feel less,
And no where, but in feign'd Arcadian scenes,
Taste happiness, or know what pleasure means."

Neither these lines in themselves nor the poem as a whole is consistent with the ideas of Crabbe, whose smugglers certainly have an aim in their actions, who

dealt mostly with the outward aspects of village life; Crabbe is concerned with its searing effects on the soul. If Crabbe's pictures emphasize the darkness at the expense of the light, they do so only the better to symbolize the internal desolation of the villagers, and only that Crabbe's essential charity may the better be expressed.

5

Although there is development in Crabbe's later writings, there is nothing in these which in any way contradicts the fundamental attitudes of *The Village*. The poet had found a way to look at life, and that world-view, as we shall see, underwent few changes through the rest of his career.

The Village was followed in 1785 by *The Newspaper*, a poem not without merit, but without great merit. The Biographer remarks that it . . .

was considered as in all respects of the same class and merits with 'The Library;' and the author was anew encouraged by the critics, and by the opinions of Mr. Burke and others of his eminent friends in London. Yet, successful as his poetical career had been, and highly flattering as was the reception which his works had procured him in the polished circles of life, if we except a valueless sermon put forth on the death of his patron, the Duke of Rutland, in 1787, and a chapter on the Natural History of the Vale of Belvoir, which he contributed to Mr. Nichols's account of Leicestershire, shortly afterwards, he, from this time, withdrew entirely from the public view. His 'Parish Register' was published at the interval of *twenty-two* years after 'The Newspaper;' and, from his thirty-first year to his fifty-second, he buried himself completely in the obscurity of domestic and village life, hardly catching, from time to time, a single glimpse of the brilliant society in which he had for a season been welcomed, and gradually forgotten as a *living* author by the public, who only, generally speaking, continued to be acquainted with the

surely did not deny feeling to the poor, and who knew perfectly well that the poor are sometimes happy, however clouded that happiness might be. I would be more ready to agree with Mr. Batdorf that Cowper's lines "at least reinforce Mr. Lang's thesis, that Crabbe's realism in the handling of rural life was a part of a movement, not a new departure," were I convinced that the lines are particularly realistic.

name of Crabbe from the extended circulation of certain passages in his early poems, through their admission into 'The Elegant Extracts.'[68]

Of these twenty-two years in the life of Crabbe we know little except what his son writes; this is pleasant reading, but not particularly important for our present purposes. The fact that he spent much time "botanizing," and that he tried his hand at novel-writing will interest us later, but need not concern us now.

The Parish Register bore many superficial, and some very fundamental, resemblances to the earlier poetry. In the first place, and most obviously, it was written in heroic couplets, which in itself served to link it with the tradition of Pope and Johnson. Crabbe's use of the couplet in narrative will briefly occupy us later; as a formal, outward appurtenance of his allegiances, however, it no doubt provided for the common reader of 1807 a convenient and accessible portal through which to approach the new poem. The couplet, at least, was nothing new. It was no doubt a feeling of the reaffirmation of the tradition of eighteenth-century poetry in an age which was witnessing more and more of what seemed to be poetical confusion that lay behind a certain amount of the praise which the reviewers accorded the 1807 poems upon their appearance.[69] Jeffrey wrote in the *Edinburgh:*

His characteristic, certainly, is force and truth of description, joined for the most part to great selection and condensation of expression;— that kind of strength and originality which we meet with in Cowper, and that sort of diction and versification which we admire in "The Deserted Village" of Goldsmith, or "The Vanity of Human Wishes" of Johnson. If he can be said to have imitated the manner of any author, it is Goldsmith, indeed, who has been the object of his imitation; and yet his general train of thinking, and his views of society, are so extremely opposite, that, when "The Village" was first published it was commonly considered as an antidote or an answer to

---

68 *Life,* p. 125.

69 For a bibliography of the contemporary reviews of Crabbe's poetry, see *Huchon,* pp. 523–525.

the more captivating representations of "The Deserted Village."
Compared with this celebrated author, he will be found, we think,
to have more vigour and less delicacy; and while he must be admitted to be inferior in the fine finish and uniform beauty of his composition, we cannot help considering his as superior, both in the
variety and the truth of his pictures.[70]

"Force and truth of description . . ." "strength and originality
. . ." "the variety and truth of his pictures . . ." are all attributes
par excellence of the poets within the satiric-realistic tradition.
We must remember, moreover, that however much Jeffrey may
have wanted to praise Crabbe, he did not have to invent the
characteristics which he commended.

Although we may safely say that *The Borough* is essentially
The Parish Register on a larger canvas, it is by no means true
that these are both merely extensions of *The Village.* Apart
from the fact that the later poems are on a much larger scale,
and that in them we do find a use of "low" details which is somewhat illusory in *The Village,* the most important difference lies
in the emphasis on character which appeared in Crabbe's poetry
after his long silence. In *The Village* the characters are all typical; individual villagers did not interest the poet. In the poems
of 1807 and 1810, however, and in all of Crabbe's narrative
verse, the interest is focused on particular characters, set in the
background of the small town which may be the ostensible subject of the verse. This growing interest in character has obvious
implications for our later discussion of Crabbe's narratives, and
at that time we shall explore the subject in some detail. Even in
these late narratives, though, the background is very often that
which was portrayed in the earlier poetry.

That background is undoubtedly Aldborough—the same Aldborough which had been the subject of *The Village,* the Aldborough which Crabbe knew as a boy and as a young "doctor"
and curate, and which, wherever in the kingdom he might
reside, whether in Suffolk itself or in Leicestershire or Wiltshire, always remained more or less the stage upon which his

[70] Jeffrey, *Contributions,* p. 276.

fictional characters played. To describe it apart from the poems in which it plays so large a part would be supererogatory. Aldborough exists today in Crabbe's poetry just as it existed in the late eighteenth and early nineteenth centuries, and we need only go to the poetry to discover its minutest physical characteristics—the church, the inns, the alms-house, the clubrooms: they are all there just as Crabbe himself knew them.

There is no reason to deny that Crabbe drew these descriptions from life, nor do I see why one should want to deny it since it is quite consistent with the tradition of which he was, by this time, the nineteenth-century representative. He himself acknowledges his debt to the external world in a note to Letter XVIII of *The Borough:*

This scenery is, I must acknowledge, in a certain degree like that heretofore described in the Village; but that also was a maritime country:—if the objects be similar, the pictures must (in their principal features) be alike, or be bad pictures. I have varied them as much as I could, consistently with my wish to be accurate.[71]

Good pictures were his aim, and his missiles hit the mark. The pictures of places and things were never more than a backdrop, however, for the life that went on in or before them, and, as I have mentioned, in *The Parish Register* and *The Borough* it is the life of individual men and women, portrayed with the same accuracy that he devoted to the almshouse, which is beginning to become Crabbe's major concern. He freely confesses to Mary Leadbeater, one of several feminine correspondents whose company he enjoyed, for the most part only through letters, during the last decades of his life, that these, too, were drawn from observation:

Yes, I will tell you readily about my creatures, whom I endeavour to paint as nearly as I could, and *dare*—for in some cases I dared not. This you will readily admit; besides, charity bade me be cautious. Thus far you are correct; there is not one of whom I had not in my mind the original, but I was obliged in most cases to take them from their real situations, and in one or two instances even to change the

71 Ward, vol. I, p. 459.

sex, and in many the circumstances. The nearest to real life was the proud ostentatious man in "the Borough," who disguised a little mind by doing great things; yet others were approaching to reality at greater or less distances. Indeed I do not know that I could paint merely from my own fancy, and there is no cause why I should. Is there not diversity sufficient in society. And who can go even but a little in the assemblies of our fellow-wanderers from the way of perfect rectitude, and not find characters so varied and so pointed that he need not call upon his imagination?[72]

Despite Hazlitt's petulant objection that "Whatever *is*, he hitches into rhyme,"[73] it goes without saying that Crabbe did not present everything there was to be seen. We have already noticed how, in *The Village*, he had taken great pains to present both sides of every coin he chose to display, but the world of even one man's observation is too enormous to permit of more than an exceedingly limited presentation, and any limitation presupposes selection. That Crabbe selected some of the more tarnished coins to place in his showcase it would be folly to attempt to deny, but a reading of *The Parish Register* and *The Borough* will quickly reveal that he had by no means abandoned his classical and realistic ideal of balanced presentation in these later works. The balance is not formal, and to that extent the strict neo-classic critic might have considered it inartistic, but it is inherent in the work, and is not there by accident. In the Preface to the 1807 *Poems* Crabbe wrote:

In the "Parish Register," he [the reader] will find an endeavour once more to describe village-manners, not by adopting the notion of pastoral simplicity or assuming ideas of rustic barbarity, but by more natural views of the peasantry, considered as a mixed body of persons, sober or profligate, and hence, in a great measure, contented or miserable.[74]

True to his word, both sobriety and profligacy, both content and misery are presented:

[72] December 1, 1816. See *The Leadbeater Papers*, London, 1862, vol. II, p. 340.

[73] *The Spirit of the Age*, vol. XI of the *Works*, ed. P. P. Howe, London, 1930, p. 164.

[74] Ward, vol. I, p. 97.

"But ever frowns your Hymen? man and maid,
"Are all repenting, suffering, or betray'd?"
Forbid it, Love! we have our couples here
Who hail the day in each revolving year:
These are with us, as in the world around;
They are not frequent, but they may be found.

[*The Parish Register* II, 384–389.]

There is no surfeit of happiness in *The Parish Register,* but the tradition of which Crabbe was the latest representative found life little more cheerful than did he. In no one of his works, however, does he lead us to believe that all of all lives is completely obscured by woe.

In *The Borough* it is the reader who is most apt to be borne down, for this poem, taken as one poem, is by all odds the most difficult of Crabbe's works to defend, even though it contains some of his most beautiful, his most elegant and pathetic passages, and in a few places approaches what fifty years earlier a critic might appropriately have termed "the sublime," although there is no particular reason to suppose Crabbe was consciously endeavoring to achieve this latter quality. As the Biographer points out, "the opinion of the leading Reviews was again nearly unanimous," upon the appearance of the poem in 1810, in "agreeing that 'The Borough' had greater beauties and greater defects than its predecessor, 'The Parish Register.'" He goes on to remark, "With such a decision an author may always be well pleased; for he is sure to take his rank with posterity by his beauties; defects, where there are great and real excellences, serve but to fill critical dissertations."[75] Some critical dissertations, we may hope, take notice of both; but however much one may prefer to dwell upon beauties, certain defects intrude themselves. Did not even so sympathetic a critic as Jeffrey have to write a long theoretical treatise in his review of *The Borough* in order to justify his pleasure in the "low" parts of the poem, despite which he was still forced to condemn outright certain whole sections—the letters on elections, professions, and trades?[76]

[75] *Life,* pp. 187–188.

[76] Letters V to VIII. Jeffrey's review appeared in the *Edinburgh* for April, 1810, pp. 30-55. See *Contributions,* II, p. 306.

It is significant that it was these particular sections with which Jeffrey took issue, because they do not enter properly into his theoretical discussion at all. In other words, he disliked them not because they were offensive, but because he thought them dull. To his judgment in this respect a modern reader will certainly in part accede, except possibly in the case of Letter VII on "Physic," rather more sprightly than the others, where the poet satirizes the medical quacks in a manner no less pertinent today than in 1810. Crabbe's justification for the inclusion of this material would no doubt have been the same as that which he introduced into his "Preface" in anticipation of cavils against his letter on "Inns": "If it describe things which we behold every day, and some which we do not wish to behold at any time: let it be considered . . . that from a Poem whose subject was a Borough, populous and wealthy, these places of public accommodation could not, without some impropriety, be excluded." It is not a very accurate justification, since it must be clear that even in 7,000 lines he had to exclude a good deal, still it serves to indicate an approach to his material more unimaginative and pedestrian than any he used before or after *The Borough*. The approach, in so far as Crabbe followed it, enormously increases the value of the work as a social document, while diminishing its stature as a poem.

As a poem, however, *The Borough* does have stature, and that not merely because of length. Strang has remarked that "If it is elevation of tone that makes *The Village* readable, it is pure glee that saves [the low] part of *The Parish Register*."[77] By this "glee" he referred to the evident joy Crabbe took in his own creative process; the same joy appears with increased intensity in his next poem. He is entranced by his surroundings; one of his greatest delights is evidently to tell us about them, and we cannot help responding. We must remember, however, that this is never a delight merely in inns and churches and other inanimate objects, for the world of Crabbe is peopled, and by the time we come to *The Borough* it is the people who absorb our interest.

[77] Strang, *Crabbe*, p. 50.

The development of Crabbe's narrative gift will briefly occupy us later. His powers as a story-teller were most fully displayed in the *Tales* of 1812 and in the 1819 *Tales of the Hall,* where his characters occupy usually a middle station in life. In the 1810 poem we find such characters also, but presented in short sketches and never, with one exception (Letter XIII), developed to such length as to engross an entire Letter, while no less than seven of the sections are devoted to seven individuals from the "lower orders." In this respect the poem represents a culmination of the interest in the poor first expressed in *The Village,* and it is a culmination entirely worthy of its first expression. The stories of poor Jachin, the parish clerk, of Ellen Orford, Abel Keene, and Peter Grimes rank not only with Crabbe's greatest achievements, but among the finer achievements of ninetenth-century literature in England. Their excellence, it almost goes without saying, lies not in the fact that they have in part to do with "low" detail, or that they were a genuine innovation in English poetry—and they were that despite the fact that Wordsworth had published *Michael* in 1800; it does not even lie in the conduct of the stories themselves as such, because the peculiar excellence of Crabbe's later narratives, the interplay of characters one upon another, has only a small part in them. Their excellence lies in the fact that in them is most fully displayed one of Crabbe's highest qualities, and one that links him most closely with the eighteenth century. It is the quality which inspired Fielding's *Enquiry into the Late Increase of Robbers* and John Howard's *State of the Prisons,* which was the impetus behind Jonas Hanway's labors for the Foundling Hospital, the Magdalen House, and the Marine Society, and at the same time one without which Johnson's noble review of Soame Jenyns' *Free Enquiry into the Nature and Origin of Evil* would have been impossible. It is a quality which is hard to define and as hard to name. Mr. Lang has called it "humanism," but although it is clearly related to the classical humanism which underlay Johnson's protest against the inanities of Jenyns, the term itself would never have been applied in the age when the Lexicographer defined a humanist as "a philologer, a grammarian."

One is tempted to call it "humanitarianism," and that is closer but still inaccurate since that word had contemporary associations with perfectibilitarianism, a doctrine which Crabbe, at least, would have been the very last to embrace. We might indeed call this quality "charity," and that will do, if we keep in mind that we mean a stoic-Christian charity—not merely almsgiving, but a desire, springing from a growing sympathy with and endeavor to understand the weakness and failures of individual men and of groups of individuals, to improve the lot of suffering mankind.[78] Possibly none of the men named above, certainly not Johnson, would have disagreed with Crabbe when, in one of his rare overt moralizations, he wrote:

> Man must endure—let us submit and pray.
>
> [*The Borough* I, 270.]

It is, indeed, perhaps only when men are able really to "submit and pray" that they can become truly charitable, for it is not until men are willing to recognize that suffering is inevitable and must be endured, just as it is not through denying the perversity of man but through an overwhelming recognition of it, that a true charity can come into being. Whatever may be the paradox implied in the line, the attitude it expresses did not impede a growing desire to see the lot of man in general improved, nor did it ever preclude an attempt at understanding, tending at times to sentimentalism, of individual men.

The emphasis upon the individual is not pronounced in Johnson, but in opposing the easy optimism of the benevolists, as Bate points out, he "continually faced and distrusted the evil and fluctuation inherent in animal nature and the empirical

---

78 Crabbe makes this viewpoint explicit in one of his unpublished sermons, the manuscript of which is at the University of Chicago Library, MS 639, p. 621. It is significant that this is the second of two sermons on I Cor. 13 which the manuscript contains. The first of these seems to have been one of his favorite sermons, for he recorded that it was delivered at least fifteen times between 1784 and 1821, exceeded in number of recorded deliveries only by a sermon on I Gal. 6, 7: "Be not deceived, God is not mocked: for whatsoever a man soweth, that shall he also reap." The second sermon on I Cor. 13 seems to have been composed for delivery in Trowbridge, on 8 July 1827.

world,"[79] and this distrust inevitably led him to the consideration of that evil as represented in the distress of particular men.
When he is refuting Jenyns' assertion that:

there is some inconceivable benefit in pain abstractedly considered;
that pain, however inflicted, or wherever felt, communicates some
good to the general system of being, and that every animal is some
way or other the better for the pain of every other animal . . . [and
just as we have] not only animals for food, but choose some for our
diversion, the same privilege may be allowed to some beings above
us. . .[80]

He turns with bitter, bitter irony to the possible manifestation
of this doctrine in individual lives:

Some of [these beings], perhaps, are virtuosi, and delight in the
operations of an asthma, as a human philosopher in the effects of the
air-pump. To swell a man with a tympany is as good sport as to
blow a frog. Many a merry bout have these frolick beings at the
vicissitudes of an ague, and good sport it is to see a man tumble
with an epilepsy, and revive and tumble again, and all this he knows
not why.[81]

In refuting Jenyns' assertion that "Poverty, or the want of
riches, is generally compensated by having more hopes, and
fewer fears, by a greater share of health, and a more exquisite
relish of the smallest enjoyments, than those who possess them
are generally blessed with," Johnson wrote:

The poor indeed are insensible of many little vexations which sometimes embitter the enjoyments of the rich. They are not pained by
casual incivility, or mortified by the mutilation of a compliment;
but this happiness is like that of a malefactor, who ceases to feel the
cords that bind him when the pincers are tearing his flesh.[82]

The man who had written that would not hastily disagree with
Crabbe, when he wrote in the "Preface" to *The Borough:*

[79] Bate, *From Classic to Romantic,* p. 71.

[80] *Review of a Free Enquiry etc. . . . .* Johnson's *Works,* 1810, vol. VIII, pp. 44–46.

[81] *Ibid.,* p. 46.

[82] *Ibid.,* p. 33.

It has always been held as a salutary exercise of the mind, to contemplate the evils and miseries of our nature. I am not, therefore, without hope, that even this gloomy subject of imprisonment, and more especially the Dream of the condemned Highwayman, will excite in some minds that mingled pity and abhorrence, which while it is not unpleasant to the feelings, is useful in its operation: it ties and binds us to all mankind by sensations common to us all, and in some degree connects us, without degradation, even to the most miserable and guilty of our fellow-men.[83]

This is a profound and noble view of the moral importance of poetry, a view rising far above mere didacticism; and yet it is a view intimately associated with that outlook upon life which Johnson and Crabbe had in common. They both had known the grimmest poverty, the most ugly humiliations which the eighteenth century afforded. Johnson wrote, "The only reason why we should contemplate Evil is, that we may bear it better,"[84] and Crabbe extends this:

> And when on Man's soft Heart these Evils press;
> The awakened Poet paints the due Distress;
> Tells how it came, and presses on the Mind
> That we are Men, and of the suffering Kind.
> We own the grieving and opprest as Friends;
> The Mind enlarges as its Grief extends;
> And Grief that's painted true improves the Heart it rends.[85]

We can be sure that these men were speaking from a deep conviction born of the distress which they were unafraid to contemplate. Johnson and Crabbe had in common a view of life which determined not to overlook the unpleasant when it is significant, for to them both suffering was an integral and not necessarily a beautiful or rewarding part of life. They refused to adopt the Pollyanna-premise. Notice that Crabbe carefully distinguishes the functions of Grief itself and of art depicting

[83] Ward, vol. I, p. 279.

[84] *Review of a Free Enquiry etc.* . . . . edition cited, p. 48.

[85] Posthumous fragment printed from MS in possession of the Cambridge University Press. Ward, vol. III, pp. 474–475.

Grief. Grief may enlarge the mind, that is, make us understand better and sympathize more fully with the griefs of others; but painted truly it improves the heart, it gives us the *charity* to act upon our understanding.

I suspect it is this refusal to compromise with unpleasant realities which has, by a curious transmutation, been called Crabbe's "disillusion," a disillusion which, as such, he has been supposed to share with the eighteenth century. Nothing can be further from the truth so far as Crabbe's art is concerned. Huchon, so far as I know, was the first writer on Crabbe to mention "disillusionment" when, discussing Crabbe's tragic tales, he wrote: "In varying degrees, a common element is to be found in the foregoing tales: the pathos of disenchantment. There is not one of their suffering heroes but has his mind shattered by the failure of his hopes. The poet of disillusion, Crabbe makes it the mainspring of his tragic stories."[86] Strang, Mr. S. J. Looker, and most lately, Mr. Lang developed the idea at some length.[87]

Now even though it is true that there was a certain aura of disillusionment hanging over the intellectual atmosphere of the later eighteenth century, it is not necessary to impute the aura to a poet whose primary concern was never with those areas to which it might be relevant. A. O. Lovejoy has shown, for example, that the eighteenth-century denunciations of pride are often expressions of a certain disillusionment of man about himself, and that the concept of the Chain of Being implied the dethronement of man from his former exalted position;[88] and Mr. Bate implies the same kind of disillusionment when he points out that the closing years of the century were characterized by the sad conviction that the essential nature of man was not reason, but either a conglomeration of habits and instincts or else, as German philosophers were beginning to reaffirm, a circum-

86 *Huchon,* p. 341.

87 S. J. Looker, "In Praise of Crabbe," *The Nineteenth Century and After,* vol. CX (1931), p. 490. See also Strang, *Crabbe,* p. 20; and Lang's article cited, pp. 316–318.

88 A. O. Lovejoy, " 'Pride' in Eighteenth-Century Thought," *Essays in the History of Ideas,* Baltimore, 1948, p. 65.

scribed ego which has little hope of knowing anything beyond its own world.[89] But Huchon and those who have followed him do not refer to this disillusionment as to the status of man in the scheme of nature or to the lowered estimate of man's ability to comprehend the world about him when they speak of the quality in Crabbe, and indeed there would be little basis for such a reference. They are speaking of the simple fact that Crabbe's favorite narrative theme in his tragic stories is the failure of an individual to attain his high promise or to achieve the happiness which has at one time seemed within possibility. The tale "Edward Shore" has been pointed out as such a story and held up as an example of Crabbe's "disillusion," but the proposition upon which the story is based and which it serves to exemplify seems to render such an interpretation doubtful:

> Evil and strong, seducing passions prey
> On soaring minds, and win them from their way;
> Who then to vice the subject spirits give,
> And in the service of the conqu'ror live;
> Like captive Samson making sport for all,
> Who fear'd their strength, and glory in their fall.
>   Genius, with virtue, still may lack the aid
> Implor'd by humble minds and hearts afraid
>
> .   .   .   .
>
> Till strong temptation, in some fatal time,
> Assails the heart, and wins the soul to crime;
> When, left by honour, and by sorrow spent,
> Unused to pray, unable to repent,
> The nobler powers that once exalted high
> Th' aspiring man, shall then degraded lie:
> Reason, through anguish, shall her throne forsake,
> And strength of mind but stronger madness make.
>
>   [*Tales* XI, 11–31.]

The idea is a perfectly straightforward one, and it is developed in a straightforward manner. It is the story of the fall of pride, of the brilliant man whose failure to recognize his

---

[89] Bate, *From Classic to Romantic*, p. 160. Bate, of course, has earlier pointed out the importance of the British empiricists to this process of "disillusionment."

limitations leads him to madness; but I do not see that it is a story of disillusionment any more than is the story in the fifteenth of the *Tales,* "The Squire and the Priest," of the squire who attempts to "raise" a young curate to his own ideas of lax living but finds, in the end, that his protégé has become a Methodist. Both the tragic and the comic tale hinge on a perception of the great incongruity between aspiration and achievement, between promise and fulfillment which is the basic fable not only of satire, but of all tragic or comic narrative. In this sense Crabbe is no more disillusioned than Shakespeare or Chaucer, both of whom, after all, wrote about Troilus and Cressida. There is absolutely nothing in "Edward Shore" of the disillusionment of which Lovejoy and Bate write. There is never any doubt as to the powers of Edward or as to Edward's importance in the scheme of things; it is the misuse of these powers and the overestimation of this importance, his overconfidence, his pride, which brings about his tragic fall.

Some writers have also found in the posthumous tale, "Silford Hall," a representation of the first disillusionment of childhood. By a somewhat strained interpretation this may be true. The story is of a boy who is sent on a mission to a nearby noble seat. Here the kindly housekeeper shows him through the castle, and shows him, incidentally, that people there may be unhappy and licentious just as they are any place else. I question, however, that this is the kind of cosmic disillusionment which Huchon and Lang try to make out that it is. Let us not forget the subtitle of this tale: "The Happy Day." The new discoveries do not disillusion the boy; they are merely new facts. Growing up is, after all, a more or less continuous process of disillusionment for most people, and there is no particular reason to think that in the case of Crabbe it was more (or less) so than for anyone else. Since the phenomenon is so nearly a universal one, it is not at all surprising that in his old age Crabbe should decide to put it into a lightly-shaded little tale, full of sympathy for childhood.

This kind of story can represent real disillusionment in art only when the artist gives evidence of regretting and cherishing beyond their due these illusions of youth; and similarly a tale such as most of Crabbe's tragic ones can represent disillusionment only if the poet shows that he has believed people to be somehow stronger and more noble than he has been forced, by truthfulness, to represent them. The stories could represent "disillusion," in other words, only if the poet had failed to separate his ideal, the ideal which he obviously still cherishes, of the inherent nobility of man, from the occasion. Crabbe's ideal remains just as true as ever, because he sees that, as an ideal, it remains valid in, and is not violated by, the world which seems to offer so many occasions to the contrary. "Charity," he says, "hopeth all things, and judgeth with an inclination to believe what it hopeth,"[90] yet he knows that people are no more noble than he has ever thought them to be. They are as they are, and he has never seriously thought them otherwise. Charity is aware of its hopeful inclination, and he is able to judge that too, for he has learned to look at life squarely, that is, *without* illusion, which is not the same thing as *dis*illusion, and which is a necessary attribute of all realistic or satiric art,[91] the concern of which, as we have noticed, is always with things as the artist sees them to be, not as he wishes they might have been.

In a sense Crabbe's very use of precise detail to record things as he sees them belies a theory as to his "disillusionment." He never fails to recognize the gloomy and miserable aspects of human existence, yet he never cries out against them, nor for one instant gives vent to the slightest feeling that mankind is being "misused," except in so far as it misuses itself. The details, in other words, in no way contradict his sense of Order, and this sense of order, as Miss Wylie has remarked, bears irrefutable testimony to the influence of the poets with whom his father made him early familiar—to the influence of Milton, Dryden,

---

90 Chicago MS 639, p. 628.

91 It may be protested, of course, that some of the writers to whom I have applied the term "realist" were, in fact, riddled with illusions of one kind or another. Pope cherished an illusion about a "Great Chain of Being." This becomes pertinent to our discussion only if the author in question decides it was an illusion. The chain of being was illusory to Crabbe, though Pope, so far as we can tell, was quite sure he was observing facts. It might be unkindly pointed out that Crabbe cherished an illusion about God; but to him it was never an illusion, even though it later became one to Matthew Arnold.

Pope, and Young—and to the tradition of which they were a part. It is by no means merely shallow optimism when Crabbe writes:

> Oh sacred sorrow! by whom souls are tried,
> Sent not to punish mortals, but to guide:
> If thou art mine (and who shall proudly dare
> To tell his Maker, he has had his share?)
> Still let me feel for what thy pangs are sent,
> And be my guide and not my punishment![92]

This is the tried belief of a poet who had been acquainted with suffering and into the texture of whose thought the inevitability of suffering had, but without the bitterness of disillusion, been interwoven. It seems to me that it would be only the most callous, or the most callow, who could not somehow admire the triumph over illusion which such an impression represents, coming as it does from a man who had more occasion than most in his own life to taste the dregs of disillusionment.

6

In this essay we have been observing some of the ways in which the poetry of Crabbe is related to the poetry and the thought of the eighteenth century. It has hardly been necessary to assemble much evidence to prove that the work of a man who was nearly fifty years old in 1800 belongs substantially to an age of which he was so clearly a part, yet the relations we have observed may be interesting reminders of Crabbe's place in literary history. There are naturally many other pertinent connections which we have had to ignore. Some of these, it is more convenient to discuss later, such as Crabbe's apparent tendency to sentimentalism, which seems at times to contradict some of what has been observed already; other traits which we might have noticed, and which are frequently attributed to late eighteenth-century poets, do not play a prominent part, though they do play a part, in the texture of Crabbe's writing. In an age which

---

[92] *Parish Register*, III, 629–634. This is also printed by Ward, vol. III, p. 496, with one slight change in punctuation, as a posthumous fragment. See also another short poem in Ward, III, p. 488.

is often remembered for its didacticism, Crabbe is very seldom overtly didactic, even though he does in his prefaces generally make clear a moral intention in terms which are unmistakably those of the tradition of which we have seen him to be a representative:

I will not assume the tone of a moralist, nor promise that my relations shall be beneficial to mankind; but I have endeavoured, not unsuccessfully I trust, that, in whatsoever I have related or described, there should be nothing introduced which has a tendency to excuse the vices of man by associating with them sentiments that demand our respect, and talents that compel our admiration. There is nothing in these pages which has the mischievous effect of confounding truth and error, or confusing our ideas of right and wrong.[93]

His turn of thought was that of the age of Johnson. The balance we have observed in his poetry is perhaps one of the most forceful bits of evidence for this assertion, and in a tale like "The Dumb Orators" where he deals with material which might have been politically controversial, he is careful to maintain the "reasonable," the non-enthusiastic attitude toward his characters, and, incidentally, to make perfectly plain his own neutral position in respect to the doctrines which he has them discuss. We should bear in mind in this connection that Crabbe was an eighteenth-century cleric, and that he had, particularly while he was rector at Muston, but also at Trowbridge, to contend with "enthusiastic" dissenters. His handling of the situation at both places was very much what we might expect of one of his temperament. It is not too much to say that although he was opposed to "enthusiasm," he was not "enthusiastically" opposed to it. Indeed in "William Bailey" (*Tales of the Hall* XIX) he perceives clearly the connection between Methodism and social unrest. He always, in his verse, in his religion, in his dealings with the practical world, strove to strike a happy mean. This is nowhere better illustrated than in a brief report from the *Bath Chronicle* for August 21, 1817, reporting the visitation of the Lord Bishop of Sarum:

93 "Preface" to *Tales of the Hall*, Ward, vol II, p. 300.

[The sermon] was preached by the Rev. and justly celebrated Geo. Crabbe, rector of Townbridge, on 1. Cor. x. 6.; and as a prose composition subtracted nothing from the fame which he has acquired as an original English bard. Commencing with a slight but masterly analysis of the nature of man, as a creature prone to oscillate in his opinions, and to push them to extremes; it exemplified the truth of his representation in a rapid, but luminous sketch of the events of ecclesiastical history, from the promulgation of the Gospel to the present moment; and inferred the necessity of preventing that prevailing tendency to religious sentiment which is, happily, so remarkable in these days, from vibrating into the wildness of fanaticism, or the darkness of superstition.[94]

If, as McDowall contends of the eighteenth century, "the main current, after all, was one of common sense and shrewd simplicity,"[95] there is no better exemplar of these traits than the man who wrote to a friend:

How Mrs. Norris and I came to associate so cordially is a mystery inexplicable on any solution except on my part, gratitude for unexpected notice, and on hers a good-natured wish to find an Author rational on general subjects.[96]

What this last remark may tell us of Crabbe's opinion of other authors with whom he had become acquainted I leave to speculation; the remark certainly shows us the light in which he thought himself, and no doubt wished to be, seen. It is the attitude which practically any eighteenth-century author would prefer that the world entertain of him.

Even though his life was prolonged almost to the accession of Victoria and the bulk of his work appeared after 1800, it is perfectly proper for us to consider Crabbe in most essential respects an eighteenth-century author. The subject of his verse was—as with the realistic-satiric poems of Pope and Johnson—men and manners, even though it was the men and manners not of London but of Aldborough; and this subject was portrayed against a realistic background such as we find again and again in eight-

94 Broadley and Jerrold, p. 183.
95 McDowall, *Realism*, p. 17.
96 Letter to Elizabeth Charter, 5 May 1815. Broadley and Jerrold, p. 82.

eenth-century verse.[97] Furthermore, the basic attitudes with which he approached his subject were closely akin to those of the age in which he was born and in which he learned his first, most lasting, and probably hardest lessons about life. The techniques he employed to cast these subjects and attitudes into verse were those inherited from his own age.[98]

It was for these reasons that his own age, and those who later treasured the poetry of that age, found in Crabbe much to admire, even though they also found things to deplore. What the critics in the later years of Crabbe's life deplored chiefly was his use of "low" detail. This, as we have seen, was by no means such a great deviation from eighteenth-century tradition as may at first appear. Mr. Bate remarks of Johnson: "It seems probable that Johnson, at least in his critical writings if not in conversation, would never have quarreled severely with the best realistic literature of the following century; for, provided he was convinced that such literature did not sanction looseness, he certainly preferred an accurate presentation of empirical or particularized nature to a completely lifeless idealization."[99] We tread precariously when we attempt to guess what an author would have thought of literature which he could never have seen, yet Johnson did read, and approve of, Crabbe's first successful venture in his own peculiar brand of realism. The early nineteenth-century objections to Crabbe were based on the predispositions of that age, not of the one preceding, and it is to the early nineteenth century that we must now turn our attention.

97 The parallel with Hogarth in this respect has been several times pointed out: by Huchon, p. 256 and p. 273, and by Lang, at some length, in his unpublished dissertation, "Some Aspects of George Crabbe's Realism," Johns Hopkins, 1938.

98 The subject of Crabbe's diction is not a particularly fruitful one. Lang, in "Some Aspects . . ." p. 168, provides a somewhat technical discussion.

99 Bate, *From Classic to Romantic*, p. 64.

2 | CRABBE
IN THE "ROMANTIC MOVEMENT"

S AINTSBURY, in his essay on Crabbe, remarks that "Johnson could never have written the passages which earned Crabbe his fame. The great lexicographer knew man in general much better than Crabbe did; but he nowhere shows anything like Crabbe's power of seizing and reproducing man in particular. Crabbe is one of the first and certainly one of the greatest of the 'realists' who, exactly reversing the old philosophical signification of the word, devote themselves to the particular only."[1] We have already discovered that Crabbe's kind of "realism" probably came as no particular shock to the readers of his day, who were thoroughly familiar with what I have called a tradition of realism; however it is perfectly true that the emphasis on details, the emphasis on the particular as opposed to the general, was on the whole a quite late development so far as eighteenth-century poetry was concerned, and that Crabbe was its most vigorous exponent and remains one of the very few poets who fully explored the possibilities it offered. But Crabbe was not taken in by his own technique, and modestly admits its limitations:

1 Saintsbury, "Crabbe," *Essays* . . . , p. 16.

"Describe the Borough."—Though our idle tribe
May love description, can we so describe,
That you shall fairly streets and buildings trace,
And all that gives distinction to a place?
This cannot be; yet, moved by your request,
A part I paint—let fancy form the rest.
   Cities and towns, the various haunts of men,
Require the pencil; they defy the pen.

[*The Borough* I, 1–8.]

Emphasis on details is not necessarily identical with emphasis on the particular as opposed to the neo-classic conception of general nature—that which is unalterably true and inherent in the very condition of the universe. In his more formal critical pronouncements at least, Johnson stoutly defended poetry as the expression of general nature, and ruggedly opposed the obtrusion of merely individual feelings into art, and his best-known exposition of this doctrine in the tenth chapter of *Rasselas* may, if with some hesitation, be taken as the ideal *credo* of a neo-classic poet, even though it was a creed which demonstrably was ignored upon occasion. Such a creed, however appropriate it may have been to the sensibilities of most of the earlier eighteenth-century public, began, by the end of the century, to cut off from poetry certain aspects of experience which a considerable number of poets felt were relevant to poetic expression. Wordsworth, for example, must be included in this group, together with Coleridge and Bowles and probably Cowper and Burns. This development the growing strain of egocentricity—to give it the most unpleasant name—observable particularly in the influences deriving from the thought which Rousseau represented, probably made inevitable, and, as Bate points out (p. 184), although Wordsworth gave lip service to the object of poetry as "truth, not individual and local, but general and operative . . . if English romantic criticism was cognizant of the universal, it tended to regard the universal as attainable only through the particular." The method of the serious poetry of high neo-classicism was to illuminate the emotions of men by the application of universal maxims which were generally received, while that of Wordsworth was to develop his general and operative truths through observation of private emotion. The difference is that between deduction and induction, and, indeed, it is not impossible that the inductive science which was beginning to dominate the popular conception of the physical universe played its part in the shift of poetic sensibility; but I have already hinted at the part that might have been played in this development by the increasing tendency of the charity, as I have discussed it, of the eighteenth century to become practical, to devote itself to the sufferings of individual human beings. There was nothing in these labors of the Magdalen House or the Marine Society of the theorizing of Mandeville or Jenyns; they were an application of the "inductive" principle that individual good could lead to general good.

Such charitable efforts were an emphasis on the particular, a concern with the individual human emotion, and with this concern the early nineteenth century was fully in accord. It is worth noticing, however, that even though Wordsworth says that: "The powers requisite for the production of poetry are: first those of Observation and Description,—i.e. the ability to observe with accuracy things as they are in themselves, and with fidelity to describe them, unmodified by any passion or feeling existing in the mind of the describer . . ."[2]—a precept which is not out of accord with what we have observed of the eighteenth-century poetic practice—he very seldom, if ever, deviates into the kind of minute description of everyday things which is noticeable in *The Parish Register* and *The Borough,* and, indeed, very seldom does he describe things "unmodified by any passion or feeling existing in the mind of the describer." Even in *Michael,* which tells a story Crabbe himself might have used, and which is certainly humble enough, there is not the intense consciousness of *Things* which Crabbe displayed in the verse written at approximately the same period. Wordsworth says of Michael:

2 "Preface" to the 1815 edition; *Poetical Works* (ed. E. de Selincourt), Oxford, 1944, vol. II, pp. 431–432.

> . . . why should I relate
> That objects which the Shepherd loved before
> Were dearer now? that from the Boy there came
> Feelings and emanations . . .

> [*Michael,* 198–201.]

We can be almost sure that had Crabbe been telling the story he would have enumerated the objects, and that the "feelings and emanations" would themselves have been subjected to orderly and precise analysis. Wordsworth, and Coleridge and the later "romantics" also, are interested in presenting the particular human being, but either, as was frequently the case, themselves, or at least a particular human with whom they could identify themselves sympathetically. This is true in *Guilt and Sorrow,* in *The Idiot Boy,* in *Michael* and *Vaudracour and Julia,* and is no less the case in the story of hapless Margaret in the first book of *The Excursion,* to name only a few narrative poems which afford some justifiable comparison with Crabbe's.

Such tentative particularization, however, is the first step toward the kind of poetry Crabbe wrote, and when we compare these poems of Wordsworth with *The Rape of the Lock* we can see that it is a big step, one which Crabbe had no more than begun to take in the picture of the distressed "hoary swain" in the first book of *The Village.* It was not until more than seven years after the publication of *Lyrical Ballads* that Crabbe was definitely to commit himself to, and go beyond, the interests, particularly in the narratives of humble life, which Wordsworth pursued in *Michael.*

The question of influences which here obtrudes itself is fortunately one which can be almost definitely settled. It seems highly unlikely that Wordsworth's verses played any particular part in the formation of the later temper of the older poet. Crabbe was sometimes amused, sometimes puzzled by the Lake Poet, in whom he eventually recognized sparks of genius,[3] but whose genius was essentially so different from his own that even had

---

3 See *Life,* p. 164.

he been one easily to be influenced it is unlikely that his own temper would have profited much by an assimilation.[4]

Wordsworth was considerably less kind to Crabbe than the older poet was to him. His disapproval—and as we shall see it was quite definite—seems to reflect not only his own sensibility, but also that of the more elite spirits of the age. Coleridge remarks:

The presence of genius is not shown by elaborating a picture; we have had many specimens of this sort of work in modern poems, where all is dutchified, if I may use the word, by the most minute touches, that the reader naturally asks why words, and not painting are used. . . . The power of poetry is, by a single word, perhaps, to instill energy into the mind, which compels the imagination to produce the picture.[5]

"Dutchification" was a criticism levelled at Crabbe again and again, and viewing the word in Coleridge's context we can easily see why it seemed appropriately applied to a poet who, by describing so accurately the very things which the Lake Poets wanted evoked, only emphasized the fact that he did not commonly use the technique of evocation. Crabbe's interest was quite as much in individual man as was that of contemporary poets, but, for the younger men, who were rebelling against certain more or less purely technical matters of language and versification, this was obscured by the fact that Crabbe's verse was so clearly representative of an older generation, as well as by the fact that Crabbe's minuteness did not, possibly, have enough of vague eighteenth-century "sublimity" to please a nineteenth-century revolutionary poet.

In so far as Wordsworth was concerned with description, he, too, was opposed to the specific:

I will conclude my notice of this poem by observing that the plan of it has not been confined to a particular walk or an individual

4 *Ibid. Cf.* the remarks of Mr. H. J. C. Grierson in *T.L.S.* XXXI (15 Sept. 1932), p. 643, where it becomes clear that Crabbe had very little active curiosity as to the "Lakists" until after 1813.

5 Coleridge, *Shakespeare Criticism* (ed. T. M. Raysor), Cambridge, Mass., 1930, vol. II, p. 174.

place,—a proof (of which I was unconscious at the time) of my unwillingness to submit the poetic spirit to the chains of fact and real circumstance. The country is idealized rather than described in any of its local aspects.[6]

This is perfectly consistent with Wordsworth's earlier criticism of Crabbe himself in a letter to Samuel Rogers, dated from Grasmere, September 29, 1808:

... I am happy to find that we coincide in opinion about Crabbe's *verses;* for *poetry* in no sense can they be called. Sharp is also of the same opinion. I remember I mentioned in my last that there was nothing in the last publication so good as the description of the Parish workhouse, Apothecary, etc. This is true—and it is no less true that the passage which I commended is of no great merit, because the description, at the best of no high order, is in the instance of the apothecary, inconsistent, that is, false. It, no doubt, sometimes happens, but, as far as my experience goes, very rarely, that Country Practitioners neglect, and brutally treat, their Patients; but what kind of men are they who do so? Not Apothecaries like Crabbe's Professional, pragmatical[7] Coxcombs, 'generally neat, all pride, and business, bustle and conceit,' no, but drunken reprobates, frequenters of boxing matches, cock-fighting, and horse-races—those are the men who are hard-hearted with their Patients, but any man who attaches so much importance to his profession as to have strongly caught, in his dress and manner, the outward formalities of it, may easily indeed be much occupied with himself, but he will not behave toward his 'Victims,' as Mr. Crabbe calls them, in the manner he has chosen to describe. After all, if the Picture were true to nature, what claim would it have to be called Poetry? At the best, it is the meanest kind of satire, except the merely personal. The sum of all is, that nineteen out of 20 of Crabbe's Pictures are mere matters of fact; with which the Muses have just about as much to do as they have with a collection of Medical Reports . . .[8]

The logic of the passage as a whole aside, so far as *The Parish Register* is concerned, this emphasis which Wordsworth placed

6 Note to "An Evening Walk," *Works,* edition cited, vol. I, p. 319.

7 Johnson's Dictionary, 1827: "Impertinently busy."

8 Ernest de Selincourt (editor), *The Letters of William and Dorothy Wordsworth:* "The Middle Years," Oxford, 1937, vol. I, p. 244.

on Crabbe's detailed description is not entirely out of place, for in that poem and in *The Borough,* which together make a considerable proportion of Crabbe's poetry, his interest in minutiae reaches its height. He was perhaps dissuaded from a further pursuit of this interest by the concern, on the whole not complimentary, of the reviewers with this aspect of his work; but there is no particular need to assume that such was the case, since the interest in narrative which was to occupy the forefront of the rest of his poetic career was already becoming explicit in the later Letters of the 1810 poem. Even a casual reading of the first two of Crabbe's major nineteenth-century productions, however, would seem to prove that they were not primarily descriptive, for although minute descriptions do form a larger percentage of the lines than in any other works Crabbe wrote, these passages serve only to give a local habitation to the people, the individual human souls, about whom the work is centered. Even in the first letter, which is the most extended descriptive passage in the poem, we have the very brief narrative of the wreck at sea, and suddenly a *person* emerges:

> See one poor girl, all terror and alarm,
> Has fondly seized upon her lover's arm;
> "Thou shalt not venture;" and he answers "No!
> "I will not"—still she cries, "Thou shalt not go."
>
> [*The Borough* I, 253–256.]

Thereafter the Borough becomes not a place, but a congregation of people, good and evil, happy and discontented, but inhabiting the Borough even though sometimes dominated by it. This is even more the case in *The Parish Register,* where, by the very nature of the plan, Crabbe focuses on human activities.

Wordsworth obviously sensed this, because he directs his criticism against what he conceives to be faults not in the description, although he calls it that, but in characterization; and his objection, it is interesting to notice, is that the characterization is so accurate that he does not grasp the character through his own experience. It is a little like objecting to a portrait because the sitter resembles nobody in Westmorland. Wordsworth's fundamental objection is the neo-classical one that Crabbe was not true to "general nature," but reports only "matters of fact," into which he has not obviously impressed his own sensitivity.

Crabbe's own object in verse was something quite different, and it seems strange that Wordsworth did not exhibit more sympathy toward it:

> Come then, fair Truth! and let me clearly see
> The minds I paint, as they are seen in thee;
> To me their merits and their faults impart;
> Give me to say, "frail being! such thou art,"
> And closely let me view the naked human heart.
>
> [*Tales of the Hall* I, 121–125.]

This, in its attention to the individual human being, is different from the neo-classical object as stated by Johnson or Burke. It is also different from the object implied by the "Preface" to the *Lyrical Ballads*, where Wordsworth says that the poet has acquired a greater readiness and power in expressing what *he* thinks and feels, and especially those thoughts and feelings which, by *his own* choice, or from the *structure of his own mind*, arise in *him* without immediate external excitement."[9] But Crabbe's stated object is not very different from what Wordsworth actually did in many of his experiments in narrative, and the latter even speaks of "my theme / No other than the very heart of man."[10] Wordsworth is seldom able, however, to achieve the almost Olympian detachment which often is characteristic of Crabbe's stories. The detachment and balance, as I pointed out in the previous essay, are classical qualities, and perhaps if the word "romantic" is to mean anything in a general sense, it might indicate the absence of that detachment and an insistence on the part of the poet upon entering his own compositions, either in his very person or at least through emotions and impressions stressed as his own and having no other

[9] *Works*, edition cited, vol. II, p. 393. The entire paragraph is significant for our purposes. Italics in the quotation are mine.

[10] *Ibid.*, p. 461. The lines are from the verses given at the end of the 1835 "Postscript."

relation to the ostensible subject which he has chosen. Wordsworth points up this attitude in a note to "Lucy Gray":

... The way in which the incident was treated and the spiritualizing of the character might furnish hints for contrasting the imaginative influences, which I have endeavoured to throw over common
life, with Crabbe's matter-of-fact style of handling subjects of the
same kind. This is not spoken to his disparagement, far from it;
but to direct the attention of thoughtful readers into whose hands
these notes may fall, to a comparison that may enlarge the circle
of their sensibilities, and tend to produce in them a catholic judgment.[11]

This note may indicate the extent to which the serious poetic
treatment of humble life remained apart from the conventions
of the time even in 1843, because on no grounds other than a
very general similarity of subject, it seems to me, would one
think of comparing "Lucy Gray" with anything by Crabbe. At
any rate, although the subject of the poem happens in this case
to be mostly Lucy Gray, the fact that Wordsworth was concerned about "spiritualizing" her would indicate that it may
be almost to the same extent Wordsworth's own mind, which
he perhaps did not clearly differentiate from "the very heart of
man." Herein, clearly, is the chief difference between Wordsworth, between at least one kind of "romantic" poet, and
Crabbe: the former never forgets himself, never really leaves
himself out of any poem; the latter goes to considerable pains
to eliminate himself from his work—this will appear more fully
in our discussion of his narratives—and to present with clear-
sighted understanding people as they actually presented themselves to him, not as his own mind transformed them. Both
poets are, in practice, interested in the particular, although the
"romantic" tended to disavow this interest in his critical remarks, and both are concerned with presenting individual human beings; but a Wordsworth poem is usually about Wordsworth, while one by Crabbe is oriented not toward the poet's
psyche, but toward the observed world.

11 *Ibid.*, vol. I, p. 346. The note is one of those dictated to Isabella Fenwick
in 1843.

But there is another difference, a difference in the attitude toward poetry which it would be difficult to point out in specific passages, but which nevertheless permeates the worlds of the two poets. The poets whom we term "romantic" felt that the poet was a man set apart from the rest of mankind, a man with superior powers and more intense intuitions, while Crabbe, so far as we know, thought of a poet as a man who wrote poetry. To say this is merely to put into concrete terms the difference implied by the different emphases we have seen above. There is no reason to believe that Crabbe was unaware of his own endowments,[12] but in Wordsworth such awareness became publicly explicit. There would be nothing more fascinating than to attempt to follow out the reasons for this change of attitude on the part of the poets toward themselves, for it is a change which to a large extent determined the poetry of the nineteenth century and is at this moment felt more strongly than ever before, but we can afford to notice only one somewhat amusing incident which does something to illuminate it.

Sir Walter Scott first records the incident in his journal, under the date of January 1, 1827:

Talking of Wordsworth, he [Huntly Burn] told Anne a story, the object of which, as she understood it, was to show that Crabbe had no imagination. Crabbe, Sir George Beaumont, and Wordsworth, were sitting together in Murray's room in Albemarle Street. Sir George, after sealing a letter, blew out the candle which had enabled him to do so, and exchanging a look with Wordsworth, began to admire in silence the undulating thread of smoke which slowly arose from the expiring wick when Crabbe put on the extinguisher. Anne laughed at the instance, and inquired if the taper was wax, and being answered in the negative, seemed to think that there was no call on Mr. Crabbe to sacrifice his sense of smell to their beautiful and evanescent forms. In two other men I should have said, 'why it is affectations,' with Sir Hugh Evans, but Sir George is the man in the world most void of affectation; and then he is an exquisite painter, and no doubt saw where the *incident* would have succeeded in painting. The error is not in you yourself receiving

12 See *Life*, p. 167.

deep impressions from slight hints, but in supposing that precisely the same sort of impression must rise in the mind of men otherwise of kindred feeling.[13]

Wordsworth himself somewhat corrects the story in a letter to Lockhart:

The anecdote of Crabbe and the candle smoke was often *told me* by Sir George Beaumont, and in the conclusion drawn from it by *him* I concurred, not so much as set down by Sir Walter that it was a proof of the Poet's *want of imagination* as of a sense of *beauty*, but I was not present when the thing occurred—whether at Murray's or elsewhere I do not recollect. "And can you see any beauty in that?" was the exclamation of Crabbe when Sir George having in vain attempted to stop his hand, gave vent to his regret for what had been done.[14]

Thomas Moore adds a note of his own in his journal:

. . . [Scott] spoke of Wordsworth's absurd vanity about his own poetry; the more remarkable as Wordsworth seems otherwise a manly fellow. Story told him by Wordsworth of Sir George Beaumont saying one day to Crabbe at Murray's, on Crabbe putting an extinguisher on a tallow candle which had been imperfectly put out, and the smoke of which was (as Sir G. Beaumont said) curling up in graceful wreaths, "What, you a poet, and do that?" This Wordsworth told Scott was a set-off against the latter's praises of Crabbe, and as containing his own feelings on the subject, as well as Sir George Beaumont's. What wretched twaddle! . . .[15]

Sir George, being an artist and a famous connoisseur, may actually have been interested in the figurations of the smoke as it curled upward, and very possibly was annoyed when Crabbe stopped it, but it seems unnecessarily discourteous to have made an issue of the incident, and the whole affair is indicative of a degree of interest in one's own sensations and a consciousness of that interest which would have been quite foreign to the under-

13 J. G. Lockhart, *Memoirs of the Life of Sir Walter Scott, Bart.*, Boston, 1862, vol. VIII, p. 167.

14 *Letters*, edition cited, "Later Years," vol. II, p. 928.

15 Thomas Moore, *Memoirs, Journal, and Correspondence* (ed. Rt. Hon. Lord John Russell), London, 1853, vol. IV, p. 335.

standing of most poets before the nineteenth century. Words-worth's concurrence in Sir George's conclusions is even more interesting. When he says, "want of imagination," I take him to mean, in part, a want of self-consciousness, whatever else may have been implied by the term; and by a "sense of beauty," may he not have meant, "a sense of one's sense of beauty"?—a sense which it was the poet's prerogative if not his duty to indulge. His reaction is easily explainable on no other basis.

The possibilities for specific parallels and contrasts between the poetry of Crabbe and that of Wordsworth in particular are numberless, but they would eventually resolve themselves into a frequent similarity of ostensible subject, which was neverthe-less turned, in fact, into different subjects by the consistently different approaches the two poets made to their material. It is this difference of approach which more than anything else kept Crabbe out of the main stream of nineteenth-century poetry.

Of Crabbe's relationships with the other poets of the early nineteenth century there is little to say which would be per-tinent to his work. By the time he met these men or read their poetry he was an old dog, and uninterested in new tricks. This is in itself admirable, for it shows a reluctance to attempt what could hardly have been otherwise than badly performed.

2

We are forced to a comparison of Crabbe with Wordsworth by the fact that they both chose subjects from humble life. Had they not this in common I am not sure we would profitably in-volve ourselves in the difficulties which such a comparison pre-sents. The fact that Crabbe frequently chose to write on sub-jects which also interested Wordsworth may easily lead, how-ever, to a basic confusion as to the motives of the older poet in choosing these subjects.

I do not know that it can ever be determined exactly why a man chooses to write the poetry he does. Crabbe wrote about his village because he knew about it, and because he wanted to dispel some more or less purely literary fancies about village life which had insinuated themselves into popular thinking and descended into mere cant. He wrote from his parish register because, again, he was thoroughly familiar with his subject, because he had enjoyed success in a somewhat similar endeavor, and because, encouraged by his success twenty-odd years before, he felt confident of his ability to handle the material. We know that in that interval of more than twenty years he wrote, experimented, and burned almost incessantly,[16] so it becomes even more significant that at the end of the period he should choose to reappear in a form which was so distinctly reminiscent of what he had earlier accomplished. *The Borough* provides the connecting link between his earlier work and the *Tales,* where his interested eye begins to penetrate more deeply into the peculiarly human problems of social living. But what underlying, perhaps subconscious, causes actually determined this series of events it is beyond the province of sane criticism to pretend to determine. We can, however, be fairly sure that he did not choose to write about humble life for the reason that Ebenezer Elliott later chose to write about it, that is, because of a specific desire to reform social inequalities. Although he fairly frequently shows a clear understanding of particular social problems, he has no theory to present and no doctrine to preach.

This has not been easy for some commentators on Crabbe to understand, for people who have social theories and doctrines are usually unsympathetic with those who have not; it thus is a little difficult for Miss Wylie, for example, to admit that Crabbe has any mind at all or any faith in the human intellect when he does not obviously make a stand on every social or political problem,[17] particularly since his artistic interests seemed to invite great "positions." It was not only his artistic interests which invited him to take sides.

Even a brief review of political and social conditions in England in the early nineteenth century would occupy too much space here; such facts as are necessary for understanding Crabbe's poetry can be presented as the occasion arises, and it is perfectly possible to enjoy that poetry and understand it fully

16 *Life,* pp. 127–128 and p. 159.

17 Wylie, *Social Studies . . . ,* pp. 81 ff.

with no knowledge at all of the particular period in which it was written. The poetry does, however, have certain clear relationships to the period, and since these relationships, if even occasionally by their negative quality, do something to illuminate Crabbe's mind and his methods of work they are worth investigating.

Since a man's social views are apt, at least in part, to be reflections of his politics, it will be instructive to glance for a moment at Crabbe's political orientation. His son gives a succinct and just summary of his father's opinions. He writes:

Perhaps the natural tendency of every young man who is conscious of powers and capabilities above his station, is, to adopt what are called popular or liberal opinions. He peculiarly feels the disadvantages of his own class, and is tempted to look with jealousy on all those who, with less natural talent, enjoy superior privileges. But, if this young man should succeed in raising himself by his talents into a higher walk of society, it is perhaps equally natural that he should imbibe aristocratic sentiments . . . in truth, I do not think Mr. Crabbe's case was an exception. The popular opinions of his father were, I think, originally embraced by him rather from the unconscious influence I have alluded to, than from the deliberate conviction of his judgment. But his was no ordinary mind, and he did not desert them merely from the vulgar motive of interest. At Belvoir he had more than once to drink a glass of salt water, because he would not join in Tory toasts. He preserved his early partialities through all this trying time of Tory patronage . . . But when, in the later portion of his life, he became still more intimate with the highest ranks of society, and mingled with them . . . and became the rector of a large town, and a magistrate, I think again, the aristocratic and Tory leanings he then showed were rather the effect of these circumstances than of any alteration of judgment founded upon deliberate inquiry and reflection. But of this I am sure, that his own passions were never violently enlisted in any political cause whatever; and that to purely *party* questions he was, first and last, almost indifferent. . . . [h]e carried his impartiality so far that I have heard him declare, he thought it very immaterial who were our representatives in parliament, provided they were men of integrity, liberal education, and possessed an adequate stake in the country. . . . He not only felt an equal regard for persons of both parties, but would willingly have given his vote to either; and at one or two general elections, I believe he actually did so.[18]

We can actually see this reluctance to take sides on party issues working itself out at least once in his verse, and at the same time we get an insight into why he himself did not become a party man. In the first of the *Tales,* entitled "The Dumb Orators," we are introduced immediately to the high-Tory Justice Bolt, "impetuous, warm, and loud," who has achieved considerable reputation in his native town as a most staunch defender of his principles in debate. On one occasion when he is in another city, he inadvertently attends a meeting of a radical club:

> Knowledge to gain and give, was the design;
> To speak, to hearken, to debate, and dine:
> This pleased our traveller, for he felt his force
> In either way, to eat or to discourse.
>
> [*Tales* I, 110–113.]

But the situation is not as he expected:

> Now, dinner past, no longer he suppress'd
> His strong dislike to be a silent guest;
> Subjects and words were now at his command—
> When disappointment frown'd on all he plann'd;
> For, hark!—he heard, amazed, on every side,
> His church insulted and her priests belied;
> The laws reviled, the ruling power abused,
> The land derided, and its foes excused:—
> He heard and ponder'd.—What, to men so vile,
> Should be his language?
>
> [*Ibid.,* 122–131.]

As a matter of fact, he is unable to decide upon any rhetorical approach appropriate to the situation. In his indecision he can only sit silently and listen in uncomfortable amazement:

[18] *Life,* pp. 167–169.

There were Reformers of each different sort,
Foes to the laws, the priesthood, and the court.

.   .   .   .

The rash were proud to blame their country's laws;
The vain, to seem supporters of a cause;
One call'd for change that he would dread to see;
Another sigh'd for Gallic liberty!
And numbers joining with the forward crew,[19]
For no one reason—but that numbers do.

[*Ibid.*, 141–150.]

That last couplet may give some hint as to Crabbe's opinion on the subject of parties. The chief agitator of the meeting is one Hammond, who, when the Justice is finally so bold as to speak, is able to draw upon the psychological advantage of being in his home territory, and routs the Tory completely.

Justice Bolt gets a chance to turn the tables, however, for some time later Hammond wanders into the Tory club of which Bolt is the mainstay, and the latter is able to defeat his opponent in precisely the same way he himself had been defeated:

As a male turkey straggling on the green,
When by fierce harriers, terriers, mongrels seen,
He feels the insult of the noisy train
And sculks aside, though moved by much disdain;
But when that turkey, at his own barn-door,
Sees one poor straying puppy and no more

.   .   .   .

He moves about, as ship prepared to sail,
He hoists his proud rotundity of tail,
The half-seal'd eyes and changeful neck he shows,
Where, in its quick'ning colours vengeance glows

.   .   .   .

Urged by enkindling wrath, he gobbling goes.
   So look'd our hero in his wrath, his cheeks
Flush'd with fresh fires and glow'd in tingling streaks. . .

[*Ibid.*, 368–385.]

19 *Cf.* Johnson, *The False Alarm,* London, 1770 (2nd ed.), pp. 38–39.

Faced with this, Hammond is forced to retire in dismay, and Justice Bolt and the Tory Party are triumphant.

Now the idea of this tale, in contrast to that of much poetry written about the same time, is clearly that nothing, really, is ever pure black or pure white. We cannot fail to notice that both Hammond and Bolt are made to look ridiculous, the Tory, if anything, more so than the Radical, as the very heroic simile just quoted shows. Bolt's final victory is certainly no more the triumph of principles than was his initial defeat in debate: the defeat and the victory were both entirely matters of chance and rhetoric.

One would think that this might have been a somewhat dangerous idea to put forth in 1812, and had the tale been told without a leavening of satiric humor, or had its thesis been put forth as an essay in a popular magazine, Crabbe might well have been a candidate for the Tower; certainly neither party would have given him help. It would be quite wrong, however, to assume from the fact that he rejected the extreme views of both parties that he was unaware of the issues involved. Crabbe's political position was the radical one, to use the term in its radical sense, of preferring good government before parties, and this position had his unwavering adherence, even, occasionally, to the point where it involved him in actual physical danger. In the general election of June and July 1818, when Trowbridge was fanatically Tory, it is typical of Crabbe's primarily agrarian orientation that he continued to support John Benett of Pyt House, who was not only a Whig but also a Protectionist—that is, he was against the reduction of duties on grain, a policy which enraged the mercantile and working people of the towns. On at least two occasions, Crabbe was assailed by a mob of his parishioners with hisses and abuse, but he only replied by "rating them roundly" and continuing to support Benett fearlessly. William L. Bowles transmitted to the Biographer a report of what occurred on election day, when he apparently was in Crabbe's company:

A riotous, tumultuous, and most appalling mob . . . besieged his house, when a chaise was at the door, to prevent his going to the poll and giving his vote in favour of my most worthy friend, John Benett of Pyt House, the present member for the county. The mob threatened to destroy the chaise and tear him to pieces, if he attempted to set out. In the face of the furious assemblage, he came out calmly, told them they might kill him if they chose, but, whilst alive, nothing should prevent his giving a vote at the election, according to his promise and principles, and set off, undisturbed and unhurt, to vote for Mr. Benett.[20]

On the other hand in 1826 he seconded the nomination of John Wilson Croker, no Whig!, who was standing for Aldborough, and who later wrote of him to the Biographer: "He was, as a conscientious clergyman might be expected to be, a church-and-king man; but he seemed to me to think and care less about party politics than any man of his condition in life that I ever met."[21] To this statement, a reviewer in the *Edinburgh Review* replied:

This depends upon what is meant by "Church-and-King." If we are to understand by them a Church Establishment and a limited Monarch, the assertion undoubtedly is nothing more than the truth; but if we are to understand the words, as most readers will presume that Mr. Croker understands them, in their Sacheverell sense, the accurate commentator on Boswell has been strangely mystified by his own zeal or by Crabbe's courtesy. The welcomer of the French Revolution was to the last a reformer of Lord Grey's school.[22]

Crabbe's own opinion of the Sacheverell "Church-and-King" clergyman is made clear by his presentation of such a one in the second of the *Posthumous Tales*:

> James was a churchman—'twas his pride and boast;
> Loyal his heart, and "Church and King" his toast;
> He for Religion might not warmly feel,
> But for the Church he had abounding zeal.
>
> . . . .
>
> "Why send you Bibles all the world about,

20 *Life*, p. 210; see also *Huchon*, p. 454.

21 *Life*, note p. 169.

22 *Edinburgh Review*, LX (1835), pp. 269–270.

"That men may read amiss, and learn to doubt?
"Why teach the children of the poor to read,
"That a new race of doubters may succeed?
"Now can you scarcely rule the stubborn crew,
"And what if they should know as much as you? . . ."

. . . .

These were his favourite subjects—these he chose,
And where he ruled no creature durst oppose.

[*Posthumous Tales* II, 125–145.]

We shall shortly have occasion to return to the views of this gentleman. The tone of the quoted passage should in itself be sufficient to substantiate the objection of the Edinburgh reviewer. It is entirely characteristic of Crabbe, too, that he should take pains to show how these views might directly affect the lives of the poor, for although he no doubt had aristocratic leanings, and even at the end of his life seems to have idealized the concept of an aristocracy quite exquisite in perception and action,[23] a concept which had certainly in no visible way repressed his own talents, he nevertheless saw clearly into the life of that class from which he had sprung. His charity was never lulled by his comfort.

It would not particularly profit us to discuss in any detail Crabbe and the French Revolution. His son records that, "He was one of the innumerable good men who, indeed, hailed the beginning of the French Revolution, but who execrated its close,"[24] but Crabbe's references in his poetry to the situation in France are of a passing nature and serve to refine his perceptions of party differences at home:

"He dared the most destructive things advance,
"And even pray'd for liberty to France;

[23] See for example *Tales of the Hall* IX, 240–250; but it is interesting that in this particular instance the conception turns out to be false, for the idolized young Lord, we later discover, is a rake just like other people. The passage has, however, a ring of authenticity which cannot be ignored and which itself is supported by the humble dedications by Crabbe of his last works to members of the Rutland family, even though such dedications were long since passé. For a discussion of this aspect of Crabbe's thought see *T.L.S.* XXXI (4 February 1932), p. 65.

[24] *Life*, p. 166.

> "Had still good hope that Heaven would grant his prayer,
> "That he might see a revolution there.
> "At this the tory-squire was much perplex'd,
> " 'Freedom in France!—what will he utter next?
> " 'Sooner should I in Paris look to see
> " 'An English army sent their guard to be.' "
>
> [*Tales of the Hall* X, 102–109.]

But although the Edinburgh reviewer may have overemphasized the importance to Crabbe of the Revolution, he was quite correct as to Crabbe's viewpoint on reform. Writing on the subject to his son in 1831, when the agitation for the Reform Bill was reaching its height and the ministry was struggling against the Lords in its support, he says, in a letter dated October 24 from Clifton, near Bristol, where he was a guest of the Hoares:

I believe there is a fund of good sense as well as moral feeling in the people of this country; and if the ministers proceed steadily, give up some points, and be firm in essentials, there will be a union of sentiment on this great subject of reform by and by; at least, the good and well-meaning will drop their minor differences and be united.[25]

His general attitude toward the last troubled twenty years of his life can probably best be summarized by another quotation from his own hand. Writing to Miss Charter on February 11, 1817, he says: "You ask my opinion of the Times. I cannot give a satisfactory one, but I dread no Insurrections, no Henry Hunts, no Cobbetts; and I hope cheerfully, and I have comfort in the Benevolence and morality of the country in general."[26]

---

[25] *Life*, p. 295.

[26] Broadley and Jerrold, p. 154. William Cobbett was a self-made man who achieved some fame both as a conservative and radical on both sides of the Atlantic; after a libel suit in 1804 he began to take the popular side in political issues, and was for a time imprisoned in the same cell as Leigh Hunt. He was best known as publisher of the radical *Political Register*. Henry Hunt would have seemed to Crabbe a more imposing figure, for in 1809 he organized a meeting in Wiltshire to thank Colonel Wardle for demanding an inquiry into the conduct of the Duke of York as Commander-in-Chief, and in order to qualify Cobbett to address it, presented him with a freehold tenement. He was perpetually engaged in lawsuits with his neighbors and with the Crown. In 1812 he was an unsuccessful candidate for Bristol against Crabbe's acquaintance, Sir Samuel Romilly, who himself was defeated. He presided in 1819 at the disastrous meeting known later as the "Peterloo Massacre." See *DNB*.

Hunt and Cobbett were men who were not taken lightly in 1817, but Crabbe's willingness to look beyond them, beyond the very real threat which to many people they offered, to the "benevolence and morality of the country" cannot, I think, be taken as evidence of an effort to avoid the issues which these radicals were agitating. Mr. Laurence P. Spingarn says of Crabbe's relationships to the problems which faced England at the time that: "Crabbe's social consciousness lies close to that of our own time, except that he was incapable of linking the effects he observed to their underlying causes. Lacking complete social insight, he never rises above awareness, but his awareness is of a high order."[27] It seems to me that this remark somewhat undervalues Crabbe's ability to seize a situation. It is true that even as late as *The Parish Register* there does appear a lack of understanding, not of the people themselves, but of some of the reasons which lie behind the deplorable situations in which the poet found them. After describing conditions in the worst part of the parish, he concludes:

> Whence all these woes?—From want of virtuous will,
> Of honest shame, of time-improving skill;
> From want of care t'employ the vacant hour,
> And want of ev'ry kind but want of power.
>
> [*The Parish Register* I, 236–239.]

To a modern sociologist this would seem naïvely to place the burden of their woes directly on the individuals themselves. They do not have the virtuous will, therefore they suffer the consequences. The last line of the quotation, implying that the people do have the power to improve themselves, but that they do not use it, is a statement of the attitude which the reader only of *The Borough* and earlier works (where no such statement is ever made) is too apt to carry away. The fact that the poet was less tolerant and understanding at this time than he later became is not altogether surprising. In 1807 he was still a country parson living, for the most part, in Suffolk, his livings

---

[27] "George Crabbe as Realist," *The University of Kansas City Review*, vol. XVII, no. 1 (Autumn, 1950), p. 63.

in Leicestershire held by a curate; he had never had the opportunity to observe and evaluate the workings of a more complex society which had developed so rapidly beyond his ken, and he relied for his interpretations entirely upon what he was able to observe in an agricultural community, or upon what he was able to remember, and very occasionally observe again, in the decadent seaport of Aldborough. In this simpler social structure it might, in fact, be somewhat difficult to understand on any basis but that of individual defections in character the phenomena of poverty. True, the enclosures had worked immeasurable hardship on the small landowners and tenant farmers, but these were having their effect in a part of England with which Crabbe was not intimately concerned, and do not play the part in Crabbe's poetry which we would expect, largely because through the 1810 publication he situated his characters in his native town, where honest fishing, supposedly, could still provide a man with bread. Having read *The Deserted Village,* he was certainly aware of the injustices worked by the enclosures, but he no doubt felt the problem too difficult and complicated to bring into poetry which was never primarily concerned with "problems" as such.[28] At any rate, the closest he comes to presenting agrarian problems is his example of the evils of absentee ownership in recounting the death of the Lady of the Hall in the third part of *The Parish Register.*

There is clear evidence, however, that when in 1814 he took up residence in Trowbridge, a manufacturing town, his viewpoint widened considerably. This, very likely, was the inevitable development of a man gifted with sharpness which,

---

[28] As a matter of fact, he may have had little occasion to bring it into his poetry, because the enclosures had hardly begun to affect Suffolk. Mr. Gilbert Slater has provided data showing that by 1801 there had been no more than ten acts of enclosure for Suffolk, affecting only 1.5 per cent of the land—and these were in a part of the county remote from Crabbe's residence. In contrast to this, by 1801 there had been 133 acts of enclosure for Leicestershire, affecting 35.5 per cent of the land. It is notable also that between 1761 and 1799 the wheat acreage of Suffolk increased slightly, while that in Leicestershire decreased by 4,000 acres. See Gilbert Slater, *The English Peasantry and the Enclosure of Common Fields,* London, 1907, pp. 140–147. It is worth considering that had Crabbe been primarily interested in social problems, he would no doubt have written about enclosures, since he must have observed them in Leicestershire.

though keen, needed tempering to discriminate. A letter to Miss Hoare, daughter of his friends at Hampstead, shows that he was quite clear in his grasp of the fundamental problem posed by industrialization; his view, in fact, was so clear that he was quite unable to accept any of the ready-made solutions which agitators were propounding. The letter is dated from Trowbridge, January 27, 1829:

Nothing has occurred at Trowbridge that indicates a combination among a great part of the Inhabitants, and the Reply given to a representation of the State of the Town to the Magistrates was One that keeps them quiet, and perhaps Watchful, but points out nothing by way of Advice or Command. I have no serious Apprehensions: true I am sorry for the want of Sufficient Work for the Willing and Industrious, and, like you, I lament the use, and still more the increase of Machinery; yet what can be done? Other Countries not so burdened with debt as we are contend with us: they also make Cloth and Birmingham Wares, and we are told that to lay aside our Inventions is to give up our Trade. God knows what will be the result of such Dilemmas, where on one side the Masters feel the necessity of employing Agents who do not eat or drink, and on the other the men who are hungry and thirsty, threaten, and no wonder, their Rival the machines with utter Destruction. Who can truly say, that if I were a master I would give up Machinery, if I were a workman I would starve in quiet? . . . A way will be found, though my Wisdom is at a loss to know where to look for it. The Mule would not be tollerated [sic] in this Neighborhood, and yet it is a sad thing to check and baffle Ingenuity, though a worse to do this by Hunger joined with a will to Labour.[29]

Crabbe's wisdom was surely little less than that exercised by the most wise of his time, but it is significant that just as in party politics he refused to commit himself to one side, so in this issue which loomed so large in the minds of serious people, he did not permit class loyalties to impair his understanding.

This increased understanding and widened observation of social problems are reflected clearly in a passage on crime as a

[29] Broadley and Jerrold, p. 293.

social problem which appears in the second of the *Posthumous Tales,* to which I have already made reference. The same James who was quoted before has this to say about crime and criminals:

> "You make your prisons light,
> "Airy and clean, your robbers to invite;
> "And in such ways your pity show to vice,
> "That you the rogues encourage, and entice."
> For lenient measures James had no regard—
> "Hardship," he said, "must work upon the hard;
> "Labour and chains such desperate men require;
> "To soften iron you must use the fire."
> Active himself, he labour'd to express,
> In his strong words, his scorn of idleness;
> From him in vain the beggar sought relief—
> "Who will not labour is an idle thief,
> "Stealing from those who will;"
>
> [*Posthumous Tales* II, 156–168.]

This no doubt clearly reflects the opinions of the "Church-and-King" men of whom we have already seen James to be a representative. It is a view of which Crabbe decidedly disapproves, and although he is not raucous in his disagreement, he patiently, and even a little sadly, makes his own insight into the problem perfectly plain:

> He knew not how
> For the untaught and ill-taught to allow,
> Children of want and vice, inured to ill,
> Unchain'd the passions, and uncurb'd the will.
> Alas! he look'd but to his own affairs,
> Or to the rivals in his trade, and theirs;
> Knew not the thousands who must all be fed,
> Yet ne'er were taught to earn their daily bread;
> Whom crimes, misfortunes, errors only teach
> To seek their food where'er within their reach;
> Who for their parents' sins, or for their own,
> Are now as vagrants, wanderers, beggars known,
> Hunted and hunting through the world, to share

Alms and contempt, and shame and scorn to bear;
Whom Law condemns, and Justice, with a sigh,
Pursuing, shakes her sword and passes by.—
If to prison we should these commit,
They for the gallows will be render'd fit.

[*Posthumous Tales* II, 168–185.]

With this passage before us, I do not know how we could be content to say that Crabbe was "incapable of linking the effects he observed to their underlying causes." He had perhaps not observed all the causes which the modern sociologist would point out, but he has a most firm grasp of the immediate psychological background of crime, a perception of the valuelessness of severe punishment when unaccompanied by an amelioration of that background, and an awareness of the importance education might play in relieving the situation. It is very doubtful if many people in England in 1830 held more advanced views;[30] but we must not overlook the fact that these views were not based on large social theories springing out of the immediate nineteenth-century context, but upon his own sympathetic, charitable observation, much tempered from the days of *The Parish Register*.

The fact that Crabbe was essentially charitable and was able to see that very often men are pushed into their devious paths by accidents for which they cannot be held responsible, never seems quite to coalesce with his firm belief that men are free agents, and it is not inconceivable that the latter belief was an impediment to his acceptance of the former. It is interesting to remember that Crabbe's favorite sermon, if we may judge by his manuscript record of the number of times it was delivered, was one on the text from I Galatians 6:7, "Be not deceived, God is not mocked: for whatsoever a man soweth, that shall he also reap." There are, however, no records of this sermon having

---

30 Among these was Sir Samuel Romilly, the degree of whose intimacy with Crabbe I have been unable clearly to determine, but who, according to *Huchon*, p. 459, suggested to Crabbe the story of "Smugglers and Poachers," *Tales of the Hall* XXI, with its protest against the severity of the game laws, and who was the subject of a short, but warm, eulogy by Crabbe upon his suicide in 1818. See Ward, vol. III, p. 439. It is perfectly possible that Romilly's preoccupation with social problems may have been one factor prompting Crabbe to think along such lines.

been used after 1814, although other sermons in the Chicago manuscript are dated as late as 1832, and it may have been that about that time, the year he moved to Trowbridge, the attitude already manifest in his literary work began more to make itself felt in his pulpit. At any period of his life, I think Crabbe would have made a separation between the cases of those who are insufferably oppressed, and those who do, for all purposes of fable and morality, choose the particular road which leads them to destruction or salvation. He does not usually in his stories probe into the ultimate reasons for the situations he presents. He starts with a given set of conditions and works from there, showing the consequences for good or evil when these are put to work by the free choice of individuals. The extent to which that choice may actually have been free is a problem which would scarcely have occurred to him—the only explicit mention of it in his works is put into the mouth of a very dubious ghost in the sixteenth of the *Tales of the Hall*—but when it did so he would undoubtedly have fallen back simply on the viewpoint of the good pastor, which avoids the issue, but which provides an unimpeachable "working morality":

> "His heart is evil," said th'impatient friend—
> "My duty bids me try that heart to mend,"
> Replied the virgin—"We may be too nice,
> "And lose a soul in our contempt of vice . . ."
>
> [*Tales* IX, 325–328.]

But certainly while Crabbe was in one good sense of the word relativistic, that is, able to see that although we condemn the vice, the man who is vicious may be helpless and worthy of our aid and pity, he was nevertheless not so far along the road to modern dogmatic relativism that he did not impute validity to man's intuition of his own free will. It was his basic thesis, the necessary moral cornerstone of Crabbe's world.

3

A minor sidelight on Crabbe's relationship to several of the "romantic" authors may serve as a springboard for a large view of his relationship to the early nineteenth century: his use of opium. The Biographer mentions the fact casually—a tone he might have been expected to adopt out of filial piety even though the full possible consequences of opium addiction seem hardly to have been commonly understood at the time he wrote despite De Quincey's famous little book. The passage in the *Life* must be quoted at length:

> My father, now about his forty-sixth year, was much more stout and healthy than when I first remember him. Soon after that early period, he became subject to vertigoes, which he thought indicative of a tendency to apoplexy; and was occasionally bled rather profusely, which only increased the symptoms. When he preached his first sermon at Muston, in the year 1789, my mother foreboded, as she afterwards told us, that he would preach very few more: but it was on one of his early journeys into Suffolk, in passing through Ipswich, that he had the most alarming attack. Having left my mother at the inn, he walked into the town alone, and suddenly staggered in the street, and fell. He was lifted up by the passengers, and overheard some one say, significantly, 'Let the gentleman alone, he will be better by and by;' for his fall was attributed to the bottle. He was assisted to his room, and the late Dr. Clubbe was sent for, who, after a little examination, saw through the case with great judgment. 'There is nothing the matter with your head,' he observed, 'nor any apoplectic tendency; let the digestive organs bear the whole blame; you must take opiates.' From that time his health began to amend rapidly, and his constitution was renovated; a rare effect of opium, for that drug almost always inflicts some partial injury, even when it is necessary: but to him it was only salutary—and to a constant but slightly increasing dose of it may be attributed his long and generally healthy life.[31]

There seem to be several possible explanations for the seizure in Ipswich.[32] The profuse bleeding may have induced anemia, with a concomitant nervous excitability, and a tendency to dizziness. Under such circumstances, particularly if he had been recently bled, a fairly brisk walk could easily have brought on

[31] *Life*, pp. 153–154.

[32] For this medical information I am indebted to Dr. Clarence A. Poor of Oakland, California.

faintness. When bleeding was stopped the anemia naturally corrected itself, while the opium, having no prolonged beneficial effect, acted in the immediate situation to produce a sense of well-being by allaying the nervousness. It is more likely, however, that the onset of vertigoes in the first place is to be explained by the possibility that Crabbe had begun to suffer from a cardiac arrhythmia, which could manifest itself in dizziness and apparent gastric distress. In combination with the artificially induced anemia, this could easily account for the fainting at Ipswich, which, with attendant distress in the lower chest or upper abdominal region, was diagnosed by Dr. Clubbe as a disease of the digestive organs. The administration of opium under these conditions might actually have had some medically beneficial results. Another possibility resides in one of the various rheumatic diseases, which are still little understood, but one of which might account for the symptoms described in the biography, as well as helping, perhaps, to explain the severe illness which Crabbe suffered after the death of his wife[33] and the tic doloureux from which he later suffered so excruciatingly. In this case the opium would probably have had no good effect except to ease somewhat the uncomfortable symptoms.

The really interesting and significant thing about Crabbe's addiction to opium—and we must conclude there was actual addiction from the son's statement about a "constant but slightly increasing dose"—is that he was able so successfully to keep it under control. Mr. Meyer H. Abrams, in his intriguing study of the effect of opium visions on the works of De Quincey, Crabbe, Coleridge, and Francis Thompson, is able to demonstrate their intrusion into only two of Crabbe's minor poems, "Sir Eustace Grey" and "The World of Dreams,"[34] and only in the latter poem, one of Crabbe's very few eccentric works, and therefore much admired, is an opium vision really central. Abrams does show, conclusively it seems to me, that the genesis of this poem lies in the poppy, and that the exact correspondence between the kind of dream Crabbe describes and those of the other authors

[33] *Life,* p. 202.

[34] *The Milk of Paradise,* Cambridge, Mass., 1934, pp. 13–21.

whom he considers can be attributed to no other factor. The recently published (1960) *New Poems by George Crabbe* was not, of course, available at the time Abrams wrote. In that volume there is at least one other poem he might have considered—a metrically and psychologically very interesting unfinished poem entitled "Where am I now?"[35]—but these three or four poems taken out of the immense bulk of Crabbe's work serve only to point up how sane and "unromantic" was the poet's use of the drug.

Opium did not affect Crabbe's life seriously, nor does it seem to have oppressed him with the dreadful torpor which so debilitated Coleridge and which De Quincey dramatizes; Huchon's ascription of his "low fever and indigestion" and his apparent general lassitude at Muston to the effects of the drug[36] is not necessarily to be accepted, particularly since he seems not to have been annoyed with such symptoms again until he reached a very advanced age.

His addiction was severe enough, however, to trouble him with strange dreams, and he was occasionally tormented at night by a set of boys who followed him and whom he was unable to beat off because they were made of leather. FitzGerald mentions that he would sometimes reply, when asked whether he had slept well, "The leather-lads have been at me again."[37] He seems to have coped with this problem with the same stoic forthrightness which characterizes so many of the more admirable figures in his tales. He certainly shows no evidence of having sought "sensation" from opium as did De Quincey.

There is no doubt that there was a great deal of sensation-seeking of one kind or another during the early years of the nineteenth century. Perhaps the tendency to violent extremes is always one of man's incipient characteristics, which under certain conditions and among certain people seems to become noticeably manifest; this is a subject which awaits study, but

35 *New Poems by George Crabbe,* edited by Arthur Pollard, Liverpool University Press, 1960, pp. 52–59.

36 *Huchon,* p. 374.

37 MS notes by FitzGerald on "The World of Dreams." See *Huchon,* p. 374, n. 5.

why it is that of the chief "romantic" poets only Keats during his short life did nothing remarkably eccentric it is not for us to determine here. Even Wordsworth and Southey, we must remember, had had their moments of youthful madness, and all the "romantics" had the wanderlust at some time in their lives—the desire to seek something new in a new environment: the desire, in other words, for new sensation. And this desire for sensation—in the broad sense of more than mere physical sensation—is a working principle behind much of their most memorable poetry.

Such a principle, or more particularly a contrast to it, brings to mind the "Preface" to *Sylvae*, where Dryden remarks: "It was objected against a late noble painter, that he drew many graceful pictures, but few of them were like. And this happen'd to him, because he always studied himself, more than those who sate to him." The "romantic" poets are in the position of this painter; they are always studying themselves, while Crabbe, true to his classical disposition, is much more concerned with drawing the recognizable likenesses which could only come from dispassionate, considered study of the world around him. It is this carefully preserved classical balance of mind which kept him from the "romantic" excesses in politics and social theory and which acted also as a brake upon his tendency toward sentimentalism. Although he did present the particular—as indeed a painter who is to produce a likeness must do—the characters in his stories nevertheless achieve universality because he deals not with passions circumscribed by local custom, however much the people themselves may be so circumscribed, not with those which were never seen before and will never be seen again, but with those which he knew to be the general experience if not of all mankind (as he would have said), at least of all who are products of that culture of which he was a part (as an anthropologist would say today). Even Gifford, the arch-neo-classic, was aware of this. He objects to Crabbe's "love of circumstantial information," which, he said, "is likely, in ordinary cases, to confound rather than inform . . . But," he continues, "when the feelings are to be questioned, and the heart is to be laid bare, the same principle leads him closely to follow up nature; and thus we are conducted step by step, to the highest point of interest. In the struggle of the passions, we delight to trace the workings of the soul . . ."[38] This was, to Gifford, not Crabbe's soul or the soul of any individual; it was the human soul. In the sense, then, that his primary concern, implicitly in the earlier works, more explicitly in the later, is with the inner life of man, Crabbe certainly approached the interests of the "romantic" poets; and in so far as he was seriously concerned with problems of social justice he was also akin to them, though to no greater extent than he was akin to certain eighteenth-century figures; but the fact that he made this inner life and this concern with social problems the subjects of his objective researches, while leaving his personal feelings, for the most part, to the reader's speculation, allies him more closely with the neo-classic and classical authors whom he admired and after whose works he formed his own technique.

[38] Review of *The Borough, Quarterly Review* IV (1810), p. 293.

3 | CRABBE
AS NATURE POET

THE use of natural description in poetry is a peculiar characteristic of neither the eighteenth nor the early nineteenth centuries—unless we continue to insist that Thomson and Collins
were really born before their time—and in certain respects
Crabbe's use of nature allies him with both. In other and more
important respects, however, it allies him with neither.

The Biographer remarks at one point that his father ". . . had
no real love for painting, or music, or architecture, or for what
a painter's eye considers as the beauties of landscape. But he
had a passion for science—the science of the human mind, first;
—then, that of nature in general; and, lastly, that of abstract
quantities."[1] The son very possibly had in mind the landscapes
of the school of Constable, and, the biography being written in
the early 1830's, it is not remarkable that the poet's deficiency
in the appreciation of "the beauties of landscape" should at that
time be pointed out as a defect of his taste, even though the
modern reader may not worry about the lack of "landscapes" in
Crabbe's poetry. Whether a "real love" for the "proper objects
of taste" would have remedied the ineptitude in "the conduct

[1] *Life*, p. 158.

of the whole"[2] which the Biographer noted as a major fault of his father's poetry is a question open to dispute. Certainly in the best of the *Tales* and in the more memorable letters of *The Borough* this fault is not an obtrusive one, and it is just these in which the reader is most aware of Crabbe's "passion for science": precisely those first two of the "sciences" which his son mentions. But it is not "nature in general"—whatever the biographer meant by that phrase—which we remember when we have laid the book aside, just as it is not mankind "in general" which is commonly the explicit subject of Crabbe's writing.

Only once, in the preface to the *Tales*, does Crabbe make any considerable pronouncement as to his own literary practice. In this preface he is primarily concerned to defend himself against the charges, which we have already noticed, by Jeffrey and, principally, by Gifford that in his meticulously accurate presentation of some of the more sordid levels of life in *The Borough*, he had offended against poetic decorum and even sacrificed the right to be called a poet. He points to the examples of Chaucer, Dryden, and Pope, and says that if the standards of his critics are to prevail, "an author will find comfort in his expulsion from the rank and society of poets, by reflection that men much his superiors were likewise shut out, and more especially when he finds also that men not much his superiors are entitled to admission." He goes on to say, ". . . I must allow that the effect of poetry should be to lift the mind from the painful realities of actual existence . . . by substituting objects in their place which it may contemplate with some degree of interest and satisfaction; but what is there in this which may not be effected by a faithful delineation of existing character?"[3] Fiction, he later points out, must have the effect of reality, and this reality depends not upon the incidents related nor the characters introduced, but upon the "manner in which the poem itself is conducted."[4]

We note here what we could easily deduce from Crabbe's works, that the poet makes no pretense to being a lyric, an inspirational, or any kind of poet other than a teller of tales. This

[2] *Ibid.*   [3] Ward, vol. II, p. 11.   [4] *Ibid.*, p. 12.

is not precisely accurate, since in his first three major works he included only incidental narrative; but we may easily perceive the narrative element absorbing more and more of his interest, until, in the last letters of *The Borough*, it has for the most part overtaken whatever other intentions he may have had. By the time of the *Tales* (1812), he was clearly a narrative poet, and with the exception of such incidental verse as "The Flowers" in *New Poems* and the remarkable "World of Dreams"—and even that is a tale of sorts—he wrote only narratives thereafter. Even his earlier, "descriptive," poems are, however, not in an important sense descriptive of natural objects, but, rather, of the manners and characters of men and of local institutions. They are "descriptive" in a sense which might, in common use, be applied to Pope's or Johnson's verse rather than to Thomson's *Winter* or Collins' *Ode to Evening*. As a matter of fact, as early as 1779 Crabbe had explicitly renounced Thomson:

> Nor shares my Soul the soft enchanting Stream,
> The lambent Blaze, that [Thomson] knew to blend
> With his Creation; when he led the Eye
> Through the [year's Verdant] Gate, the budding Spring;
> And from the Willow o'er the tuneless Stream,
> And from the [Aspen] Rind, ere yet her Leaf
> Unfolding flicker'd, and from limpid rills
> Unmantled, cull'd Simplicity and Grace.
>
> [*Midnight*, 85–92.]

This poem is, incidentally, apparently Crabbe's only essay in blank verse until 1822, when he attempted, fairly successfully, narrative blank verse in "In a Neat Cottage," now published in *New Poems*. However, *Midnight* is interesting not only for this reason, but also because it combines with an experiment in "graveyard" poetry such early indications as the following of what was to be some of Crabbe's best and most characteristic material:

> The Sea-Bird sleeps upon yon hoary Cliff,
> Unconscious of the Surge that grates below

The frozen Shore; and Icy Friendship binds,
As Danger Wretches Destitute of Soul,
The wave-worn pebbles, which the ebbing Tide,
Left with the Salt-Flood shining; dark is now
The awfull Deep, and O'er the Seaman's Grave
Rolls pouring, and forbids the lucid Stream,
That silvers oft the way, a shining Beast,
Spring from the scaly people's putrid Dead,
Hanging unhers'd upon the Coral Bough . . .

[*Midnight,* 187–197.]

Ten lines of Crabbe's sampling of one poetic taste of his day is quite enough; certainly no one will be sorry that he rejected this mode.[5] It was almost thirty years before he found his artistic métier in the poetic tale, but in the meantime he had written almost all of those poems by which he is commonly remembered today. However, even though Crabbe did not make extensive use of nature in his three most important non-narrative poems—nor in his later poetry either for that matter—the relationships which he bears to the age of Johnson on the one hand, and to some of the "romantics," particularly Wordsworth, on the other, become more apparent when we consider the rôle of nature in his works.

[5] Despite his disavowal of Thomson, the poem incorporates one distinctly Thomsonian passage (lines 237–247):

"Alas! how chang'd the Verdure of this [Scene],
How lost the Flowers, how winter-struck the Blade!
No more the wild Thyme wings the passing Gale
With Fragrance, nor invites the roving Bee
To taste its Sweets—and why this direful waste
Of Verdure? why this Vegetable Death?
Did all with Man commit mysterious Sin?
All in rebellion rise?—and tepid Meads,
And Lawns irriguous, and the blooming field,
And Hills, and Vallies, and intangling Woods,
Spurn GOD's Command and Drink Forbidden Dew?—"

Another passage somewhat reminiscent of Thomson is found in "The World of Dreams," XIII and XIV. It is to be remembered that this poem is also in a verse form unusual with Crabbe, a stanza of eight octosyllabic lines rhyming ababbcbc. The significance of the verse should not, however, be exaggerated. *Cf.* "Sir Eustace Grey" and, in *New Poems,* "Hester," tales not unlike Crabbe's others in content (though the former contains a remarkable dream passage), but cast in stanzaic form,

2

With Wordsworth Crabbe did have in common his use of the more humble levels of society as subjects for sympathetic poetic treatment, but the similarity, for our present purposes, ends there. Not only did Wordsworth draw his characters from pastoral life as opposed to Crabbe's use of those from a seaport village, but in his most memorable poems he placed those characters, frequently, in a setting of sympathetic nature—a nature which seems actively to influence them, or from which they somehow derive spiritual strength. Crabbe's use of nature is almost neutral in this respect; or else, as in "The Lover's Journey," it is precisely the opposite of Wordsworth's practice. That is, Crabbe shows how the states of mind of his characters change, for them, the aspects of nature.

Another way in which Crabbe's use of nature is distinct from Wordsworth's, and distinct at the same time from a great deal of eighteenth-century writing about nature, is his common avoidance in the first place of "the sublime," and in the second, of organized landscapes or "prospects." Of the latter he no doubt could have provided more examples had he had many occasions to do so; so far as "the sublime" is concerned, he seems consciously to have avoided it. His only efforts to describe any of the larger aspects of nature concern the sea, and even then he does not feel entirely comfortable:

> Turn to the watery world!—but who to thee
> (A wonder yet unview'd) shall paint—the sea?
>
> [*The Borough* I, 163–164.]

The fact that he does paint the sea is significant when we observe how he does it. The eight lines following this couplet are, except for the last of them, couched in the most general language:

> Various and vast, sublime in all its forms,
> When lull'd by zephyrs, or when roused by storms;
> Its colours changing, when from clouds and sun
> Shades after shades upon the surface run;

Embrown'd and horrid now, and now serene,
In limpid blue, and evanescent green;
And oft the foggy banks on ocean lie,
Lift the fair sail, and cheat th'experienced eye.

[*The Borough* I, 165–172.]

Then, however, he confines his gaze, and the next sixteen lines turn into an organized seascape:

Be it a summer-noon: a sandy space
The ebbing tide has left upon its place;
Then, just the hot and stony beach above,
Light twinkling streams in bright confusion move,
(For heated thus, the warmer air ascends,
And with the cooler in its fall contends);[6]
Then the broad bosom of the ocean keeps
An equal motion, swelling as it sleeps,
Then slowly sinking; curling to the strand,
Faint, lazy waves o'ercreep the ridgy sand,
Or tap the tarry boat with gentle blow,
And back return in silence, smooth and slow.
Ships in the calm seem anchor'd; for they glide
On the still sea, urged solely by the tide;
Art thou not present, this calm scene before,
Where all beside is pebbly length of shore,
And far as eye can reach, it can discern no more?

[*The Borough* I, 173–189.]

The sea had a particular fascination for Crabbe. He speaks of it as "that first great Object of my Admiration and indeed the first of my Notice. I was an Infant Worshipper of its Glory. . . ."[7] We then need not be surprised that he should portray it, as Mr. Spingarn says, "with a distinction that a Turner might envy."[8] It is only surprising that he does not do so more often. The

6 Huchon, in quoting this passage, relegates lines 177–178 to the bottom of the page with the following note: "In characteristic fashion Crabbe feels bound to explain the phenomenon scientifically, and this piece of conscientiousness results in two intolerably prosy lines which spoil the whole passage." *Huchon,* p. 265. In this Huchon follows Sir Leslie Stephen.

7 Broadley and Jerrold, p. 217. Letter to Elizabeth Charter, 14 Sept. 1818.

8 Spingarn, *UKCR* XVII, p. 61.

storm which follows the passage just quoted is a real one, and conveys, as aptly as so few words could do, the force and majesty of a turbulent sea. We can imagine how Wordsworth or Thomson would have concluded the passage. The description would probably have led them somehow to a series of reflections upon man and the universe. Not so Crabbe. The human troubles—a shipwreck—appear in his poem, but not until the reactions of birds have first been described, and the only moral reflection with which he favors us is contained in the lines:

> And lo! the sailors homeward take their way;
> Man must endure—let us submit and pray.
>
> [*The Borough* I, 269–270.]

On at least three other occasions Crabbe had use for ocean storms, but then he only sketched them in the roughest outlines.[9]

A suspicion that Crabbe prefers the more intimate, less "sublime" faces of nature is confirmed as a fact by a further examination of his passages descriptive of natural scenes. He almost invariably describes not a "prospect" but a selection of details which he never unites, or else he limits himself to portraying the smallest possible area. "Seek, then, thy garden's shrubby bound . . ." he writes, and in another passage:

> "To dream these dreams I chose a woody scene,
> "My guardian-shade, the world and me between;
> "A green inclosure, where beside its bound
> "A thorny fence beset its beauties round,
> "Save where some creature's force had made a way
> "For me to pass, and in my kingdom stray.
> "Here then I stray'd then sat me down to call,
> "Just as I will'd, my shadowy subjects all!"
>
> [*Tales of the Hall* VII, 130–137.]

Notice that it is a "guardian shade, the world and me between" to which the Elder Brother retreats for his dreaming, not a hill with a wide view, or a heath, or the seashore, any one of which

---

[9] *Tales of the Hall* IV, 467–476; V, 424–425 and 447–450. *Posthumous Tales* IV, 111–120.

might have been the preferred dreaming-place of another poet. This is, to be sure, a part of the Elder Brother's fictional character, but it is nevertheless significant that, for dreaming purposes, he was placed by the author in a particular situation which contained none of those more majestic or awful aspects of nature which conventionally inspired so many of Crabbe's 1819 contemporaries and their followers and which, to them, would have been more appropriate to the Elder Brother's "romantic" temperament.

This abstention from the "sublime" and preference for that within reach of his hand probably bears some relationship to Crabbe's own scientific turn of mind. He had a lifelong interest in botany and entomology, and, in his later years, was fascinated by fossils. W. J. Massingham quotes Canon Ainger to the effect that Crabbe was enough of a botanist to have added some forty species of plants to those known in Suffolk.[10] In 1795 he wrote "The Natural History of the Vale of Belvoir" in *The History and Antiquities of the County of Leicester,* and his son records that in one of those "grand incremations," which so delighted his children and which were held outdoors "not in the chimney, for the bulk of paper to be consumed would have endangered the house,"[11] he destroyed an "Essay on Botany in English; which, after he had made great progress in it, my father laid aside in consequence merely, I believe, of the remonstrances of the late Mr. Davies, vice-master of Trinity College Cambridge . . . who, though little tinged with academical peculiarities, could not stomach the notion of degrading such a science by treating of it in a modern language."[12] The result of this scientific interest is sometimes almost too readily apparent in his verse:

> Eager he looks, and soon, to glad his eyes,
> From the sweet bower, by nature form'd arise
> Bright troops of virgin moths and fresh-born butterflies,
> Who broke that morning from their half-year's sleep,

10 W. J. Massingham, *Untrodden Ways,* London, T. Fisher Unwin, 1923, p. 198.
11 *Life,* p. 127.   12 *Life,* p. 128.

To fly o'er flow'rs where they were wont to creep.
  Above the sovereign oak a sovereign skims
The purple Emp'ror, strong in wing and limbs:
There fair Camilla takes her flight serene,
Adonis blue, and Paphia, silver queen;
With every filmy fly from mead or bower,
And hungry Sphinx, who threads the honey'd flower;
She o'er the Larkspur's bed, where sweets abound,
Views ev'ry bell, and hums th'approving sound;
Poised on her busy plumes, with feeling nice
She draws from every flower, nor tries a floret twice.

[*The Borough* VIII, 73–87.]

This is charmingly done and in itself is pleasant enough, but
it is versified entomology, and is not very skillfully worked into
a letter entitled "Trades."

His preference for nature at close range is further exhibited,
and an interesting question raised, by the following quotation:

He rode to Ripley through that river gay,
Where in the shallow stream the loaches play,
And stony fragments stay the winding stream,
And gilded pebbles at the bottom gleam,
Giving their yellow surface to the sun,
And making proud the waters as they run.
It is a lovely place, and at the side
Rises a mountain-rock in rugged pride;
And in the rock are shapes of shells, and forms
Of creatures in old worlds, of nameless worms,
Whose generations lived and died ere man,
A worm of other class, to crawl began.

[*Tales of the Hall* XIII, 5–16.]

Edmund Blunden's comment on this passage is worth quoting:

All our memories of the brooks in Anglia, making "washes" across
the sandy cartways, are brought to their brightest in the first part of
the passage, and we may well suppose that another sort of fancy or
personality would have gone on with the delightfulness of that little
river; but Crabbe the geologist (and obviously the geologist cares
nothing for the parson) cannot be long excluded. . . . He is true to

himself and he records his train of thought, ending with his ambiguous definition—is it satirical, is it merely scientific?—of the human being. And is this, in an artistic consideration, a false note? Those who live with Crabbe as he remains in his book will be less inclined to think so.[13]

Agreeing to the delightfulness of the passage, we may still wonder about the definition. If it is satirical, it is just a little *gauche,* for it does not represent Crabbe's working viewpoint of man; if it is merely scientific, it does seem artistically out of place, for as a generalization it is neither very original nor striking. It shows, at any rate, how this scientific interest—for whether the definition is intended to be a scientific observation or not, it certainly had its inception in Crabbe's interest in science— can sometimes play the poet false. But we must also give this turn of mind credit for the minute and vital observation of the "gilded pebbles" in the water, which gives the passage its appeal.

It is clearly impossible to make any reasonable assessment of the role his scientific mind played in contributing to or detracting from the artistic success of Crabbe's poetry, because it is impossible to imagine any other kind of mind writing the poetry Crabbe's produced. It is not "science" which was responsible for the peculiarly refreshing quality of the butterfly passage itself, depending as it does upon the euphonious scientific names—yet also, we must notice, poetic and imaginative names —of the insects. The lambent dulness of Erasmus Darwin is never present in Crabbe; the moments when he is most like his unfortunate predecessor in the versification of science, are also frequently the moments when he is most readable. So far as I know, for another example, no other poet has celebrated the beauties of a jellyfish, yet Crabbe does so twice, and each time entrancingly:

> Now is it pleasant in the summer-eve,
> When a broad shore retiring waters leave,
> Awhile to wait upon the firm fair sand,
> When all is calm at sea, all still at land;

[13] Introduction to *The Life of George Crabbe* by his Son, London, Cresset Press, 1947, p. xix.

And there the ocean's produce to explore,
As floating by, or rolling on the shore;
Those living jellies which the flesh inflame,
Fierce as a nettle, and from that its name;
Some in huge masses, some that you may bring
In the small compass of a lady's ring;
Figured by hand divine—there's not a gem
Wrought by man's art to be compared to them;
Soft, brilliant tender, through the wave they glow,
And make the moonbeam brighter where they flow.

[*The Borough* IX, 77–90.][14]

We remember these passages as among Crabbe's best not only because of their own intrinsic quality but also because of the contrast in subject-matter with the greater body of his verse, which deals with quite other affairs. They are not the most significant use Crabbe makes of nature, as Paul Elmer More was aware when he wrote: "Of this inanimate lore of plants and rocks Crabbe is most prodigal in his verse, but, by some true gift of the Muses, it never for a moment obscures the human interest of the narrative. After all, it was man, and the moral springs in man, that really concerned him."[15]

As in a discussion of any other aspect of Crabbe's work, it is to man and his moral springs that we must turn eventually to see the relationship of that aspect to the whole. As I have pointed out in another connection, Crabbe's descriptive passages never exist exclusively for themselves, for his world is peopled, and it is the people who are his chief concern.

In all of *The Village*, for example, there is only one short passage which makes an extensive use of nature imagery:

Lo! where the heath, with withering brake grown o'er,
Lends the light turf that warms the neighbouring poor;
From thence a length of burning sand appears,
Where the thin harvest waves its wither'd ears;
Rank weeds, that every art and care defy,

14 The other example is *The Borough* XXIII, 325–326.

15 Paul Elmer More, "Genius of Crabbe," *Shelburn Essays*, 2nd Series, New York, 1907, pp. 131–132.

Reign o'er the land, and rob the blighted rye;
Where thistles stretch their prickly arms afar,
And to the ragged infant threaten war;
There poppies, nodding, mock the hope of toil;
There the blue bugloss paints the sterile soil;
Hardy and high, above the slender sheaf,
The slimy mallow waves her silky leaf;
O'er the young shoot the charlock throws a shade,
And clasping tares cling round the sickly blade;
With mingled tints the rocky coasts abound,
And a sad splendour vainly shines around.

[*The Village* I, 163–178.]

This passage is striking and memorable (and it was possibly more striking to the reader of 1783 than to us today), and, indeed, it must be so, for it forms a sort of scenic back-drop for the tableaux which Crabbe is to present. Holme refers to Crabbe's "constant choice of the less pleasing parts of a landscape for minute treatment,"[16] and, even though it is clearly not true that Crabbe's choice of these parts of the landscape is "constant," particularly in the later works, it is an attestation of the force of a few descriptions such as this that he should remember them as being practically omnipresent in the poetry. The back-drop remains throughout the performance, although it is pointed out to us only at curtain-time.

That the back-drop in this case, as through most parts of the three earlier important poems, is a gloomy one cannot be disputed. "Withering," "burning," "thin," "blighted," "prickly," "ragged," "sterile," "slimy"—adjective after adjective drives home to the reader the picture Crabbe wants him to keep in mind. The only flowers blooming are those that "mock the hope of toil"; the only plant "hardy and high" is the mallow, and the "young shoot" is shaded by wild mustard. The splendor is vain and sad. It is completely beside the point that, as Woodberry, with his late Victorian prejudices as to the nature of beauty, remarked, "there is loveliness in a salt marsh," and

16 J. W. Holme, "Treatment of Nature in Crabbe," *Primitiae: Essays in English Literature,* By Students of the University of Liverpool, Liverpool, 1912, p. 44.

probably untrue that "Crabbe could not present it, nor even see it for himself."[17] Woodberry happened to be referring to a description in "Peter Grimes," but for our purposes the situation is the same: if Crabbe does not in this instance present the loveliness of the scene, it is because that loveliness is not to his artistic purpose. The details he presents are carefully selected with the tone and subject of the poem and its effect upon the reader in mind. In other words, to carry on with our mid-twentieth century prejudices as to the nature of beauty, by his selection of these particular details Crabbe is not only setting the scene for the entire poem, but subtly inducing the reader to adopt a mental "set" from which to approach the remainder of what he has to present. The poet has completed his introduction—the prologue to the succeeding tableaux—in which he has stated that he paints "the Cot / As Truth will paint it, and as Bards will not," and now he presents us with the first and most plainly visible truth, the natural surroundings of the village— the stage back-drop, which hints to us what we may expect from the remainder of the performance.

The question of some sort of interaction between "nature" and the other elements of the poem does not become prominent in *The Village,* nor, indeed, in *The Parish Register.* Crabbe uses a few lines at intervals throughout the poem to recall the initial picture of the natural surroundings to our minds,[18] but these surroundings are, in themselves, not the subject of his discussion, and he gives us no clear indication of what part he thinks external nature plays in the lives and thoughts of the characters he introduces, beyond the obvious implication that because here "Nature's niggard hand / Gave a spare portion to the famished land" the people inhabiting that "frowning coast" will suffer for Nature's niggardliness.

The first letter of *The Borough* bears almost the same relationship to the whole of that poem as the lines we have been

17 G. E. Woodberry, "A Neglected Poet," *Studies in Letters and Life*, New York, 1891, p. 44.

18 *The Village* Book I, 109; 131–132; 150; 200–205; possibly 321–322.

discussing bear to *The Village*.[19] It is, however, more than a poetical back-drop, since actual incident, and interaction between men and nature, occurs in the lines devoted to a storm and shipwreck. The background is, however, only in part the sea, even though it is in writing of it in this letter that Crabbe, as we have seen, produces some of his best description. The lines from line 163 to the end of the letter are probably among the most memorable pictures of the sea in English literature, but that element does not play quite the important part in the ensuing poem which this first "General Description of The Borough" would lead us to expect. The fault is not a very important one, but it is a small example of the "deficiency in the conduct of the whole" of which the Biographer speaks.

The technique of presenting the natural setting at the very beginning of the poem is a simple and not very subtle one, and since Crabbe uses it only seldom in poems after *The Borough* it is pleasant to believe that he outgrew it, if it was ever an essential part of his technical apparatus. Crabbe's subjects do not in general require a natural background and, as a matter of fact, his method of describing natural scenery does not readily lend itself to use in providing one. This is true because he very seldom presents us an entire, organized scene; he does not as a rule write "landscape" poetry.

The question of "landscape" poetry as such is, I think, one which need not long detain us. The fact that Crabbe did not in this respect follow the footsteps of Thomson, Dyer, and others is in him neither a singularity nor necessarily a deficiency. When he wants to present a scene organized pictorially he does so very effectively,[20] but he ordinarily had no occasion for such pictures, and made his nature passages serve quite different purposes.

If one has the impression of a "landscape" after reading the lines quoted from *The Village,* it is because he has himself

19 And, incidentally, it bears approximately the same arithmetical proportion to the whole: about one-thirtieth.

20 For example *Tales of the Hall* XIII, 701–724, quoted later in this essay.

organized the objects presented into a coherent scene. We have at least a heath, apparently in the foreground, and a length of "burning sand" "Where the thin harvest waves its wither'd ears," but the "rocky coasts" are in a completely unspecified relationship to these. The poet has almost entirely confined his attention to the sickly plants, indeed, to specific species. These plants the reader can see clearly, but not in any organized way as growing upon a heath (or upon the "length of burning sand" —we do not know positively where we are looking through most of the passage). The description is one which gives us, rather than a literally pictorial back-drop for the tableaux—if we may revert to our earlier metaphor—an *impressionistic* one such as scenic designers for the modern ballet frequently provide. Since Crabbe presents no coherent scene which can be grasped in its entirety, it is the mood and attitude conveyed to us by the description of these unhappy vegetables which are important to the poem. The same situation prevails in his other works. In the use of nature to prepare his scene or to illuminate the occurrences thereon, Crabbe is a master, giving just the proper touches, emphasizing precisely the detail which we recall later as important for his purposes, yet never allowing an obviously genuine pleasure in writing of nature to divert him from his main design.

3

Crabbe was too much concerned with human beings and their tragedies and comedies, and too little considered any cosmic significance these dramas might have had, to have devoted very much effort to thinking through a "theory of nature." Not being a Deist, he would be naturally disinclined to accept the idea that nature is in itself a revelation of divine attributes, and he had none of the enthusiasm for the act of contemplating nature, displayed by Thomson, which might have led him to evolve an original theory. But there is what we could call a theory of perception underlying many of Crabbe's nature passages, a theory generally only implied, but stated at least once, and made then the chief matter of one of his tales:

> It is the soul that sees; the outward eyes
> Present the object, but the mind descries;
> And thence delight, disgust, or cool indiff'rence rise:
> When minds are joyful, then we look around,
> And what is seen is all on fairy ground;
> Again they sicken, and on every view
> Cast their own dull and melancholy hue . . .

> [*Tales* X ("The Lover's Journey"), 1–7.]

This theory, which, as Mr. Holme remarks,[21] anticipates Ruskin on the Pathetic Fallacy, is worked out in the tale by detailed references to nature. A lover rides to meet his mistress, traversing, and, in the anticipation of delight, reacting to barren and desolate countryside:

> For now he pass'd through lanes of burning sand,
> Bounds to thin crops or yet uncultured land;
> Where the dark poppy flourish'd on the dry
> And sterile soil, and mock'd the thin-set rye.
> "How lovely this!" the rapt Orlando said;
> "With what delight is labouring man repaid! . . ."
>
> .   .   .   .
>
> The lover rode as hasty lovers ride,
> And reach'd a common pasture wild and wide;
> Small black-legg'd sheep devour with hunger keen
> The meagre herbage, fleshless, lank, and lean;
> Such o'er thy level turf, Newmarket! stray,
> And there, with other *black-legs* find their prey.
> He saw some scatter'd hovels; turf was piled
> In square brown stacks; a prospect bleak and wild!
>
> .   .   .   .
>
> "Ay, this is Nature," said the gentle 'squire;
> "This ease, peace, pleasure—who would not admire?"

> [*Tales* X, 48–75.]

The lover sees in nature only the reflection of his own state of mind. It is beautiful when he is happy; but the aspect changes profoundly when he finds his mistress has gone to visit a friend, and he is forced to ride after her, convinced that she has be-

---

[21] Holme, *op. cit.*, p. 52.

trayed him. He goes a different route, through rich and idyllic countryside, which, however, he again imbues with his own emotion:

> Forth rode Orlando by a river's side,
> Inland and winding, smooth, and full and wide,
> That roll'd majestic on, in one soft-flowing tide;
> The bottom gravel, flow'ry were the banks,
> Tall willows, waving in their broken ranks;
> The road, now near, now distant, winding led
> By lovely meadows which the waters fed;
> He pass'd the way-side inn, the village spire,
> Nor stopp'd to gaze, to question, or admire;
> On either side the rural mansions stood,
> With hedge-row trees, and hills high-crown'd with wood.
> And many a devious stream that reach'd the nobler flood.
>   "I hate these scenes," Orlando angry cried,
> "And these proud farmers! yes, I hate their pride.
> "See! that sleek fellow, how he strides along,
> "Strong as an ox, and ignorant as strong;
> "Can yon close crops a single eye detain
> "But his who counts the profits of the grain?
> "And these vile beans with deleterious smell,
> "Where is their beauty? Can a mortal tell?
> "These deep fat meadows I detest; it shocks
> "One's feelings there to see the grazing ox—"
>
>   [*Tales* X, 232–253.]

The conclusion of the tale is most interesting. The lover finds that his mistress has not betrayed him, and that she had absented herself from the appointed meeting-place through necessity, not by her own desire. She agrees to ride back with him the next day.

> Home went the lovers through that busy place,
> By Loddon-Hall, the country's pride and grace;
> By the rich meadows where the oxen fed,
> Through the green vale that form'd the river's bed;
> And by unnumber'd cottages and farms,
> That have for musing minds unnumber'd charms;

And how affected by the view of these
Was then Orlando—did they pain or please?
    Nor pain nor pleasure could they yield—and why?
The mind was fill'd, was happy, and the eye
Roved o'er the fleeting views, that but appear'd to die.

[*Tales* X, 336–346.]

Then Orlando returns again over the same road which he
had found so pleasant in the first part of the tale:

Then could these scenes the former joys renew?
Or was there now dejection in the view?—
Nor one or other would they yield—and why?
The mind was absent, and the vacant eye
Wander'd o'er viewless scenes, that but appear'd to die.

[*Tales* X, 355–359.]

This view of the perception of nature as a reflection of a
state of mind might easily have been expanded into a full-blown
psychology, and it has obvious relationships with the empirical
philosophy of the late eighteenth century, but the country parson was not a philosopher, and with him it was a matter-of-fact
result of his artistic concern with the observation of people
rather than with ideas or things. It is in relation to this view
that almost all the nature passages in the later poetry appear.
That passage already quoted from "Delay has Danger," *Tales
of the Hall* XIII, is an exception, to be sure. Crabbe occasionally indulges (one almost says "indulges himself") in a kind of
purely objective description which is unusual because it is not
closely integrated with the matter of the tale he is telling. But
later in the same book we find this passage:

Early he rose, and look'd with many a sigh
On the red light that fill'd the eastern sky;
Oft had he stood before, alert and gay,
To hail the glories of the new-born day;
But now dejected, languid, listless, low,
He saw the wind upon the water blow,
And the cold stream curl'd onward as the gale
From the pine-hill blew harshly down the dale.

> On the right side the youth a wood survey'd,
> With all its dark intensity of shade;
> Where the rough wind alone was heard to move,
> In this, the pause of nature and of love,
> When new the young are rear'd, and when the old,
> Lost to the tie, grow negligent and cold—
> Far to the left he saw the huts of men,
> Half hid in mist, that hung upon the fen;
> Before him swallows, gathering for the sea,
> Took their short flights, and twitter'd on the lea;
> And near the bean-sheaf stood, the harvest done,
> And slowly blacken'd in the sickly sun;
> All these were sad in nature, or they took
> Sadness from him, the likeness of his look,
> And of his mind—he ponder'd for awhile,
> Then met his Fanny with a borrow'd smile.
>
> [*Tales of the Hall* XIII, 701–724.]

This description has been quoted before in essays on Crabbe; it is surely one for which no English poet would need to apologize. We might analyze it as a "prospect"—one of the very few which Crabbe wrote—for certainly the fact that the scene is organized for us may contribute something to its high quality; but it is more interesting still to observe how the scene, at least so far as the tone and mood are concerned, is not, and is explicitly pointed out not to be, a representation of whatever might actually have been there. It is in this sense a fabrication of the character's mind.[22]

In addition to the two instances already discussed, Crabbe takes pains on at least four other occasions specifically to point out this relationship between man and nature.[23] It may have been to this idea that Blunden refers when he says that Crabbe challenged certain theories of nature and of beauty current in

[22] I take the "or" in the fourth line from the end as meaning "or rather." If it is read as meaning "or else" the argument is somewhat weakened but not disastrously so.

[23] *The Borough* XIX, 272–273; *Tales* XIII, 411–412; *ibid.*, 509–510; *Posthumous Tales* VI, 86–87.

1819.[24] Since it is the soul that sees, the soul, a private organ, may see beauty in places and under circumstances which a systemized and purely aesthetic judgment could not defend. So far as scenes in nature are concerned, Crabbe indeed does this; he is able to find the loveliness to which Woodberry refers in quite unlikely places,[25] and although he did not so use it, he might have used this theory of perception (if so slight a thing can be dignified by so formidable a term) as a defense of his occasionally somewhat unlikely subject matter.

There is, however, a question as to whether Crabbe was consciously challenging anyone else's theories, as Mr. Blunden implies. Crabbe seems never to have had more than the most casual interest in literary or philosophical theories of any kind, and rather than seeing this idea as a challenge, it is more consistent with Crabbe's known character and artistic practice to regard him as simply being true to his own experience, and having no concern with its possible theoretical applications. The idea that nature derives its peculiar affective qualities from the spectator himself is, as I have already implied, not one which would seem to require much philosophical justification. Each of us can call upon his own experience to confirm the observation that "the outward eyes / Present the object, but the mind descries," for we are, if we stop to consider, aware of the discrepancies between our varying reactions to the natural objects which we encounter daily.

These statements and his general practice, do not, however, seem at first glance to coincide with what appears to be a "working theory" in some of his finest descriptive passages. Among these is the famous description of the marsh in "Peter Grimes," a passage worthy of the special praise for which it is usually singled out:

> When tides were neap, and, in the sultry day,
> Through the tall bounding mud-banks made their way,

[24] Blunden makes such an assertion, though without indicating clearly upon what he bases it. Possibly he was referring to the challenge implied by Crabbe's use of "low" detail. *Op. cit.*, pp. xix–xx.

[25] See, for example, *The Borough* IX, 161.

Which on each side rose swelling, and below
The dark warm flood ran silently and slow;
There anchoring, Peter chose from man to hide,
There hang his head, and view the lazy tide
In its hot slimy channel slowly glide;
Where the small eels that left the deeper way
For the warm shore, within the shallows play;
Where gaping muscles, left upon the mud,
Slope their slow passage to the fallen flood:—
Here dull and hopeless he'd lie down and trace
How sidelong crabs had scrawl'd their crooked race;
Or sadly listen to the tuneless cry
Of fishing gull, or clanging golden-eye:
What time the sea-birds to the marsh would come,
And the loud bittern, from the bull-rush home,
Gave from the salt-ditch side the bellowing boom.
He nursed the feelings these dull scenes produce,
And loved to stop beside the opening sluice;
Where the small stream, confined in narrow bound,
Ran with a dull, unvaried sadd'ning sound;
Where all presented to the eye or ear
Oppress'd the soul with misery, grief, and fear.

[*The Borough* XXII, 181–204.]

The last two lines of this quotation appear to be a contradiction of the thesis Crabbe was later to expound in "The Lover's Journey." It is what is "presented to the eye or ear" itself which oppresses, and not the mind's observations. The contradiction is more apparent than real, and would not long detain us were it not pertinent to more important matters. Whether or not Crabbe had a well-organized theory of nature he was a sensible man, and would have been the last to argue that some scenes, for instance a salt-marsh on a sultry day, could not just in themselves be oppressive. *Why* is a question which he did not, nor need we, discuss. But we would have a better basis for argument if the passage stood as a poem by itself, for we must keep in mind, in dealing with quotations, that we are constantly removing them from their context, and that nature, in Crabbe's poetry, always plays some part in a human world. His descriptions are never merely descriptions, but passages in a poem.

This particular passage is preceded by one almost as fine but very seldom quoted:

> Thus by himself compell'd to live each day,
> To wait for certain hours the tide's delay;
> At the same times the same dull views to see,
> The bounding marsh-bank and the blighted tree;
> The water only when the tides were high;
> When low, the mud half-cover'd and half-dry;
> The sun-burnt tar that blisters on the planks
> And bank-side stakes in their uneven ranks;
> Heaps of entangled weeds that slowly float,
> As the tide rolls by the impeded boat.
>
> [*The Borough* XXII, 171–180.]

And the salt-marsh passage is shortly followed by another which is significant for our purposes:

> A change of scene to him brought no relief;
> In town, 'twas plain, men took him for a thief:
> The sailors' wives would stop him in the street,
> And say, "Now Peter, thou'st no boy to beat;"
> Infants at play, when they perceived him, ran,
> Warning each other—"That's the wicked man;"
> He growl'd an oath, and in an angry tone
> Cursed the whole place and wish'd to be alone.
>
> [*The Borough* XXII, 209–216.]

With these three passages before us it is possible to consider them together as forming no contradiction to the plan of "The Lover's Journey." The tone of the salt-marsh passage is revealed as being quite clearly the reflection of what Crabbe, the omniscient author, wishes us to think was going on in Peter's mind. Peter was compelled to live alone with the views which to him had become dull; and since he himself was "dull and hopeless" and, we must remember, was himself oppressed by "misery, grief, and fear," the natural surroundings only accentuated these emotions, which would never have occurred to another person, however dull or sad he might have found the scene. The emotions which oppress Peter are completely inconsistent with what the scene itself could inspire, just as were the emotions of Orlando in "The Lover's Journey." If we read the passage as meaning, literally, that the "dull scenes" *produced* the emotions of "misery, grief, and fear" then neither Peter's final guilt-madness nor the poem as a whole makes any sense.

This discussion has been more than a matter of firing cannon at gadflies, for it gives a solid basis for pointing out some facts of primary importance about Crabbe's poetry. Crabbe places Peter Grimes in the dull solitude of the salt marsh, and there, amid the desolation symbolizing his state of mind, Peter is gradually overcome by his consciousness of guilt and sin until nature itself seems to breed the demons which haunt him. The natural surroundings themselves are morally neutral; it is what Peter transfers to them from his own mind which is significant for the story.

A similar, almost symbolic, use of nature (it is doubtful if Crabbe would have considered it symbolic) occurs again in "Ruth," *Tales of the Hall* V, where a storm on the coast is made the milieu of the heroine's suicide after she has determined that such is the only way to reconcile with duty to her father the revulsion she feels for the man she must marry. Crabbe apparently makes his use in this case quite explicit:

> " 'But O! what storm was in that mind: what strife,
> " 'That could compel her to lay down her life? . . .' "
>
> [*Tales of the Hall* V, 450–451.][26]

Now a poet who is so seriously concerned with the inner world of his characters will feel little desire to express *himself* à la Wordsworth in what we commonly think of as "nature poetry." In other words, it is Crabbe's concern with "the faith-

[26] Again in *Tales of the Hall* XIV, 206–209, where there is an explicit parallel between nature's and man's decay, there are hints of symbolism, but, I should say, only hints; for the passage, very beautiful in itself, could more properly be considered an oblique description of human decay rather than as presenting symbols of it.

ful delineation of existing character," with particular men and their individual problems—a "romantic" interest if one must categorize it—and at the same time his very classically objective approach to the delineation of these beset mortals which keeps him from being a lyric or a "nature" poet.

4

There is very little variation in the quality of Crabbe's nature-writing throughout his career. We may think to find a more relaxed, reflective tone in the later passages, and it is possible that he chose in the later years to describe more pleasant aspects of the natural scene than had earlier been his wont; but on the whole he not only continues to use nature with about the same infrequency, but his manner of writing about it remains almost constant once he has found the tradition within which he was to work.

It is to that classic-realistic tradition which we have discussed that we must ultimately turn if we are to see Crabbe's nature-writing in its proper perspective, for the men of the eighteenth century whose shadows glide wherever we look in Crabbe's poetry would all, to some extent at least, have agreed with Johnson's remark that "a blade of grass is always a blade of grass whether in one country or another. . . . Men and women are my subjects of inquiry." To this attitude is certainly to be attributed the fact that Crabbe, who wrote nature poetry very well, wrote so little of it. Here also may we look to account for the fact that, as Paul Elmer More remarked, he "tends to distinguish . . . sharply between men and nature rather than to blend them in any haze of symbolism."[27] Crabbe may draw instructive lessons by a parallel with nature,[28] but he neither tries to learn from nature nor in any way identifies himself, as the poet, with nature. He has not the slightest inclination either to deistic transcendentalism or toward the pantheistic belief in

[27] More, "Genius of Crabbe," p. 134.

[28] As in *Parish Register* II, 372 ff. See also *Tales of the Hall* VIII, 257–264. This usage is, of course, in the center of the tradition with which Crabbe is associated.

immanence which so many men of the nineteenth century shared. Nature existed for him as apart from, though influencing, man; as an object for pleasant contemplation, but not in and for itself a fit object for art.

In respect to his use of nature, then, Crabbe did work outside two important poetic tendencies of his time. He can be identified neither with the writers of "prospect poems" such as *Grongar Hill,* nor with poets such as Thomson and, later, Wordsworth, who used nature as a medium for the expression of philosophical ideas. Although his delight in certain aspects of nature is occasionally reflected in his poetry, we can point to no single passage in his verse with the assurance that in those lines we have the quintessential expression of that delight. Crabbe is by no means a "nature poet," even if, as Mr. Leavis remarks, "in the use of description, of nature, and the environment generally, for emotional purposes he surpasses any Romantic."[29] Mr. Leavis has his own predispositions, but even he would hardly dispute that not only are Crabbe's nature passages few, but when he introduces a passage embodying a description of external nature, that passage is subordinate, and clearly subordinate, to the "manner in which the poem itself is conducted."

A literary "if" is even more futile than an historical one, but the critic may find amusement in his fancies. It is not too much to say that *if* Crabbe had not been so much a part of the eighteenth-century "realistic" tradition, he could have been a nature poet in the commonly accepted sense of the word, for he had the requisite powers had he chosen to use them. The fact that he was not a nature poet may cast an illuminating glow, if only faintly, upon some of the puzzling ways in which neo-classical poetry operates. The mind attuned to the world as it is (however it may be), the mind of the "realist" in art, prefers to deal with the world on its own terms, not on terms imposed upon it by an imaginative, or creative, extension of the artist's own sensibilities. All art in the twentieth century has, either in its

29 F. R. Leavis, *Revaluation: Tradition and Development in English Poetry,* New York, 1947, p. 128.

very creation or at least in its interpretation, been subjected to this "romantic" egocentricity. Such an operation may lead to richer and more complex art (though I think not necessarily so, for classical art is rich and complex as the artist sees richness and complexity in the world he deals with, not merely as he imposes the convolutions of his own spirit upon not always tractable material), but it is not the mode of Dryden, Pope, or Johnson. Nor, as we have seen, is it the mode of Crabbe, whose interest finds its full expression in his narrative verse. He was not really happy writing descriptions, for nature was to him important in poetry only in its relation to the primary fact of the world in which man lives—man himself.

4 | CRABBE
AS NARRATIVE POET

MEN and the deeds of men were ever Crabbe's happiest subjects. We have already observed how the inclination of the eighteenth century turned eventually to the observation of particular individuals, and it would seem, then, a logical step to incorporate these observations in the form of narrative. This, indeed, was done in prose fiction, which had had a more or less continuous history extending back at least as far as the later Elizabethans, but it was not until the early nineteenth century and in the work of Crabbe that the realistic concerns of the tradition of Pope and Johnson manifested themselves in genuine verse narratives with any pretensions to seriousness.

Too much emphasis might easily be placed upon Crabbe's narrative poetry as the end-product of a development, the course of which we shall very briefly trace below. If we were to be able to speak with any accuracy of the development of a poetic genre, we would have to be able to produce a body of other, contemporaneous, examples of the kind of thing Crabbe did in his *Tales,* and such examples appear only very sparsely: a few examples in Wordsworth are the only things really comparable. In respect to poetic narrative, Crabbe is to be compared with no other poet in English except Chaucer, if only from the standpoint of the quantity of such verse reflecting the manners of his time. In that time Crabbe is unique, even though there was an unbroken tradition of metrical narrative extending throughout the hundred years preceding his major works.[1]

The eighteenth century was not an age of narrative poetry, despite the fact that the century delighted in stories, as the popularity of *Gulliver, Pamela,* and *Tom Jones* attests; yet the short narrative poem, similar in tone and often in style to Chaucer's *fabliaux,* was one of the most popular genres of the time, if its frequent appearance in miscellanies, and the fact that some of the more eminent poets of the early century condescended to experiment with it, may be taken as any test.[2] I have already mentioned in the first essay Swift's *Baucis and Philemon,* which is representative of the form: short, usually in tetrameter couplets, and telling a story leading almost invariably to a surprise ending. Not infrequently it was somewhat prurient, although not necessarily so. Gay was the author of at least five of these little stories in verse, and Prior also produced several of them. We may safely assume that Crabbe was familiar with these, if only because he twice mentions Prior, once in a note to *The Borough* and again in a letter to Elizabeth Charter, where he explicitly points to one of Prior's tales.[3] What occurred between Prior and Crabbe is best summarized by Mr. Draper:

Without recognition from neo-classic criticism and only by sufferance of the respectable, the stream of English narrative verse continued during the eighteenth century, continued either by bowing

[1] See John W. Draper, "Metrical Tale in XVIII-Century England," *PMLA*, XLII (1937), p. 390.

[2] See, for example, vol. II of *Pope's Miscellany,* 6th edition, 1732, which contains six of them by Dr. King, and vol. IV of *Dryden's Miscellany* for 1716, where seven such tales appear anonymously. See also Dodsley's *Collection of Poems,* 1766, vol. III, p. 183; vol. V, p. 213, p. 221; vol. VI, p. 246, p. 306. Also *The Foundling Hospital for Wit,* No. I, 1743, p. 50; No. VI, 1749, p. 73; and *The New Foundling Hospital for Wit,* 1784, vol. V, p. 123, p. 169; vol. VI, p. 120. This citation makes no pretense to be exhaustive.

[3] Broadley and Jerrold, p. 91. See *The Borough,* a note to line 339 of Letter XXIV.

to the didactic demands of the moralists or by boldly following a course outside the purlieus of cultivation and propriety. The love for story remained . . . Much more of it doubtless existed than has survived in print. During the century, however, as the rigor of the Rules and the severity of Puritanism declined, metrical tales appear more and more in thin quartos and in respectable published "Works. . . ." Thus the tale emerges by degrees from eclipse; but, as it does so, the fabliau type seems to disappear, perhaps at the price of increasing respectability, and Romantic illusion displaces the sharp piquancy of the earth earthy. The number of metrical tales in the century is considerable; and they comprise a literary corpus of some historic interest because they lead to the outburst of narrative poetry about the beginning of the next century, and also because they produced a number of realistic pieces, the poetic counterparts of Fielding's novels, that illustrate the story-telling of the tavern and the hearth, and portray the life of the period as it was lived.[4]

As to the relationship of Crabbe to this development, two things are important: first, the fact that these short narratives of the eighteenth century were never, so far as I can discover, favored by being considered as serious productions, worthy of such serious criticism as Jeffrey and others bestowed upon Crabbe; and, second, the fact that what we have called "low" detail, the minute description of everyday scenes and objects, was already fixed by convention upon narrative verse. As a matter of fact some of Crabbe's specific interests and subject matters are anticipated as early as 1713 by Swift's "Phillis; or the Progress of Love,"[5] a story which is worth a brief examination:

> Desponding Phillis was endued
> With every talent of a prude:
> She trembled when a man drew near;
> Salute her, and she turned her ear . . .

Yet Phillis knew how to bite her lips to make them red, and in the church

[4] Draper, *op. cit.*, p. 397.

[5] Swift, *Works*, New York, 1859, vol. I, p. 251.

> Would lift her eyes up to the ceiling,
> And heave her bosom unaware
> For neighbouring beaux to see it bare.

Her father makes arrangements for her marriage, but on the wedding-morning it is discovered that she has eloped with the butler, leaving a letter explaining that a fortune-teller had foretold that she was to marry a serving-man, and that since marriages were made in heaven there was nothing to be done but hope for forgiveness:

> Away they rode in homely sort,
> Their journey long, their money short;
> The loving couple well bemired;
> The horse and both the riders tired:
> Their victuals bad, their lodging worse;
> Phyl cried! and John began to curse:
> Phyl wish'd that she had strain'd a limb,
> When first she ventured out with him;
> John wished that he had broke a leg
> When first for her he quitted Peg.

Phillis was forced to break her marriage-vows to support them:

> When food and raiment now grew scarce,
> Fate put a period to the farce,
> And with exact poetic justice;
> For John was landlord, Phillis hostess;
> They keep at Staines the Old Blue Boar,
> Are cat and dog, and rogue and whore.

The reader of Crabbe will instantly find a familiar note here, for although the octosyllabic couplet gives the narration more speed, which in turn supports the much lighter tone than that which Crabbe would have given the story, the outline is one which the later poet would have delighted to use.[6] This is the nearest approach to anything like one of Crabbe's stories which I have discovered in earlier eighteenth-century literature, and the similarities are significant; but even more significant are

[6] See also Swift's "Stephen and Chloe," *ibid.*, p. 318, and "The Journal of a Modern Lady," *ibid.*, p. 295.

the differences, for although there is psychological perception of a high order present in Swift's piece, the reader of Crabbe misses the much more analytical tone, the sympathy, and the elevation which he would have supplied the theme. The poem is definitely a minor piece, almost a *jeu d'esprit,* with the emphasis entirely on the humor and the irony of the situation, rather than on the play of human emotions. As with all comic tales, a twist of the pen could have changed it into tragedy (or perhaps sentimentality), and this was the turn which it remained for Crabbe to give material which was already at hand. That Crabbe was able to take this step is perhaps due partly to the fact that he was for twenty years isolated from the intellectual and literary society of the Capital, that he was thus away from the fashions and predispositions of the metropolis—a situation which would have been intolerable for a more volatile spirit. He did not accustom himself to any new poetic styles, which may or may not have been a good thing, but at the same time he was faced with no hindrance to the development with perfect integrity of his own peculiar gifts.

2

The two decades between the publication of *The Newspaper* and the 1807 edition of the *Poems,* which contained *The Parish Register* and a number of shorter new poems in addition to his previously published works, were in no sense of the term years of inactivity. Not only was Crabbe actively employed in his parochial work, but he seems to have written constantly, if we may judge by what the Biographer reports of the material which was destroyed. Most interesting from our present standpoint is the fact, reported by his son, that during this period— in a space of two winters—Crabbe managed to bring to completion no less than three novels. The termination of his efforts in prose fiction, as reported in the Biography, is worth our attention. George Junior writes:

I forget the title of his third novel; but I clearly remember that it opened with a description of a wretched room, similar to some that are presented in his poetry, and that, on my mother's telling him frankly that she thought the effect very inferior to that of the corresponding pieces in verse, he paused in his reading, and, after some reflection, said, 'Your remark is just.' The result was a leisurely examination of all these manuscript novels, and another of those grand incremations which, at an earlier period, had been sport to his children.[7]

It is highly significant that at the end of this long interim he should choose to reappear in a form which was so distinctly reminiscent of what he had accomplished twenty years earlier, for I cannot but believe that the interim was very necessary to Crabbe's future success. In the first place, as we have just seen, he was experimenting with other forms of literature as well as with other meters (see "The Hall of Justice" and "Sir Eustace Grey"); he was finding precisely where his genius lay. But more than this, he was developing the self-confidence necessary to enable him to pursue with such singleness of artistic purpose that course which he had discovered to be for him the best. We must not forget that in 1785 Crabbe was only a country boy. He was a country boy who was a duke's chaplain, who had visited with Sir Joshua Reynolds and Dr. Samuel Johnson, and who was under the protection of Edmund Burke, but he was, or he felt himself to be, a rustic all the same. When he came from beneath the poetical wing of Burke, he seems to have been most unsure of his own abilities, and it was only at the urging of friends no less eminent than Charles James Fox, who was very soon to be prime minister, and in order to meet pressing financial difficulties, that he was persuaded to publish his 1807 *Poems*. In the "Preface" to this volume he acknowledges almost with obsequiousness his literary debts to Charles James Fox (who had meanwhile died), to Henry Fox, Lord Holland, who seems to have offered some trifling suggestions of his own, and to the Rev. Richard Turner of Great Yarmouth, of whom he says, "What altogether to expunge and what to improve he has repeatedly taught me, and, could I have obeyed him in the

[7] *Life*, p. 159.

latter direction, as I invariably have in the former, the public would have found this collection more worthy its attention."[8]

Crabbe was also preparing himself in another way for his most important work. In the 1816 Biographical Account, previously quoted, he says of these years:

Why our author should so long abstain from any call or claim upon public favour, it is not our business to inquire; but it is most probable that the subject itself, viz. Village Manners, . . . and the further opportunities which he had of viewing these in the different places wherein he resided, gave hope of success in this attempt. He must have acquired some knowledge of men and their manners; and if from disuse his facility of versification was somewhat abated, his powers of discrimination, and his accuracy in describing, were proportionately augmented.[9]

The earlier works were those which a young man could have written; the later pieces, with their detached understanding, their shrewd observations into the ways of humanity, were, I think, not. We can easily imagine that he was expressing a favorite posture of his own when he much later wrote:

> Much it amused me in the place to be
> This harmless cypher, seeming not to see,
> Yet seeing all—unnoticed to appear,
> Yet noting all; and not disposed to hear
> But to go forth—break in on no one's plan,
> And hear them speak of the forsaken man.
>
> [*Tales of the Hall* XX, 50–55.]

Upon being complimented upon the pleasant seclusion of his house and garden at Trowbridge, he replied that he preferred to the finest natural scene walking in the streets, and observing the faces of the passers-by,[10] and it is perfectly clear that a very great deal of such observation provides the tissue and the substance of his later poems.

Crabbe developed slowly, however, and the difference be-

---

8 Ward, vol. I, p. 96.

9 George Crabbe [poet], "Biographical Account . . ." cited, p. 516.

10 *Edinburgh Review* LX, no. 121, p. 252.

tween *The Village* and *The Parish Register* is not nearly so great as the foregoing remarks might lead one to suppose, even though in the latter poem we do first begin to see the author's observations taking the form of narrative. *The Village* contains only one very brief passage which might possibly be considered oriented to the form of a story—the pathetic little vignette of the "hoary swain" in lines 180 to 225—but in *The Parish Register* we find more than twenty short tales, each one more extensive than that in the earlier poem.[11] Some of these, for example that of Phoebe Dawson, a 116-line story in the second part of the poem, attracted much attention in 1807, and are still considered among the most moving things Crabbe wrote. The subject of the poem as a whole, therefore, was no longer the mere surroundings of human life, but the human figures themselves. A reviewer in the *Quarterly* in 1901 (Heathcote Statham) called these "a gallery of portraits such as very few writers in the language have equalled in variety, keenness of insight, and power of delineation,"[12] and he is correct in a way he had perhaps not quite intended, for the "portraits" are exactly that. While they are not static descriptions of the standing figure—the tales of Phoebe Dawson and Isaac Ashford, two out of many examples, present capsule life histories—they do concentrate upon the single individual, and more upon what happens to him than upon what he does. The element of the human will is by no means ignored, as the skilfully varied "Then fly temptation youth; refrain! refrain!" appearing as a sad exhortation through the story of Phoebe Dawson sufficiently proves; but the very brevity of the stories hinders the poet in the development of his gifts in searching the will, and there is never space enough at all for him to show the conflict of wills, the human elements acting one upon the other, which is the power and the interest of his later work. The large framework

[11] The number of these tales could be definitely fixed only after a tedious discussion of what exactly would constitute a narrative. Some cases are doubtful, for example the story of "Andrew Collett," Part III, 75–125. For our purposes the distinction would not be particularly useful, since there are a number of distinct and developed stories, with beginning, middle, and end.

[12] *Quarterly Review*, vol. CXCIII, p. 30.

within which he committed himself to write his poem—a pastor's recollections as he surveys the records of births, marriages, and deaths in his parish register—did in itself inhibit more expansive writing in individual sections, but of course there is no reason to believe that had Crabbe desired to write expansively he would have chosen that particular frame.

That Crabbe did not, at the turn of the century, feel himself ready to indulge in extended narrative writing is further indicated by his performance in *The Borough,* that enormous, almost amorphous *comédie humaine* (and it is so very nearly in Balzac's sense) containing some of Crabbe's best, and much of his worst, writing. Here we can trace very clearly the course of Crabbe's development as a narrator, particularly if we assume that the poem was written more or less in the order in which Crabbe finally arranged it. If we accept the growing interest in narrative as a development in technique, we are safe in making the assumption of order, for in the course of the poem we can watch the art of story-telling absorb more and more of the poet's concern. We have already noticed the very brief introduction of people into the first, primarily descriptive Letter; after this there is hardly a section of the poem which, however much primarily descriptive matter there may be, does not focus its attention upon events in the human world.[13] In the second Letter, "The Church," there is a little tale of the mourner in the churchyard, which is scarcely a narrative at all, but which serves nevertheless as an exemplum for Crabbe's exhortation, "Regard the dead, but to the living live;" a note by the poet to this line indicates that he, at least, considered the preceding matter a story. In Letter III we have extended portraits of both the vicar and his curate, neither really narratives in the sense that anything in particular happens, but astute and understanding, and containing, as nothing before has quite contained, the elements which will appear in Crabbe's later character portrayal: that is, the clear representation of both men as mixtures of weakness and strength. In almost all subsequent letters there

[13] Letters X, XVIII, and XXIII may to some extent be exceptions.

are one or more stories, and in Letter VIII, "Trades," we have one with the introduction of two characters as equal partners in the narrative, with the interest, as in so many of Crabbe's most mature tales, centering in the relations and the contrast between them. In Letter XII, "Players," the second of the two stories contained in the section almost completely loses sight of the ostensible subject of the Letter, and serves rather as an excuse for a narrative of a faulty character, servant to the passions which finally bring it to destruction.

In Letter XIII there is the quite extended story of Sir Denys Brand, who was responsible, much to his own glory, for the founding of the borough Alms House, and this story explicitly unites the stories in the next three Letters of three individuals who, through Sir Denys' favors, were admitted to the institution. In the fourteenth Letter we have for the first time an entire section of one of Crabbe's works devoted to one narrative, and this, indeed, is only a part of the implicit unity imposed upon Letters XIII to XVI. Now this kind of cyclical development had already begun in *The Parish Register* and will be carried to artistic fulfillment in *Tales of the Hall*,[14] but here it is already full-blown in conception. At this point in *The Borough* we realize that we have to deal with a narrative poet, and when we read through the first of the series of four Letters entitled "The Poor of the Borough," a possible lingering doubt is dispelled, for this cycle is the high point of Crabbe's early narrative style and the culmination, the logical extension, of those interests first displayed in *The Village*.

Each of them is an engrossing personal history; each is moving, and in its way terrible, for Crabbe can see that it is no less a human soul in jeopardy when Jachin, the parish clerk, forfeits his for a few shillings than when Barabas is lost for all the

---

14 See Horst Bär, *George Crabbe als Epiker*, Leipzig, 1929, for a full and highly technical discussion of this aspect of Crabbe's work. Bär bases his discussion upon the thesis, with which I feel constrained to disagree, that Crabbe's technique is essentially that of the epic. But see his definition of the typical epic situation, p. 11: "Ein einzelner unterhält in einer behaglichen Stunde eine nicht allzu grosse Gesellschaft durch die Erzählung eines Geschehens, dass zur Zeit der Erzählung abgeschlossen ist." It is upon this basis alone that he calls Crabbe "ein Epiker."

wealth of Malta. Peter Grimes haunted by the spectres of his crimes is in this respect no less terrible a figure than Macbeth. "Ellen Orford" and "Abel Keene" are somewhat less imposing. The former barely keeps clear of the treacherous borderlines of sentimentality (some would see it as having crossed them), and the latter in its dependence for final effect upon the terrors wrought by Calvinistic "enthusiasm" upon a weak and foolish nature no doubt seems today much less impressive than it did in 1807 simply because its subject is of less moment. All we can say when we lay it aside is "Poor, silly Abel," and that is not quite enough, even though we recognize the astuteness and insight with which the character is drawn.

But effectively written and moving as these stories are, they represent only one step in Crabbe's narrative technique, for in each of them, and in each of the longer stories in *The Borough,* Crabbe devotes his entire attention to the one figure, and other persons in the tale are only satellites. The incidents and the individual characters stand out more clearly than in anything Crabbe had previously written; the stories are structurally much more complete in themselves and the couplets become more flexible and appropriate for narration and dialogue; but, taken as a whole, they lack the penetration, the third dimension which the later narrative efforts achieve. The reason for this is that Crabbe's most powerful gift lay in the analysis of the relationships between two or more people, and no matter how deeply he probed into the mind of an individual—and I feel that it would be difficult to probe more perceptively than he did into Peter Grimes and Abel Keene—there is still only depth and length, so to speak, but not the breadth which gives some of the later tales so much substance.

Jeffrey, in his review of *The Borough,* pointed out that Crabbe "has great talents for narration; and that unrivalled gift in the delineation of character, which is now used only for the creation of detached portraits, might be turned to admirable account in maintaining the interest, and enhancing the probability of an extended train of adventures."[15] When the *Tales* appeared in 1812 they turned out to be not exactly the tales Jeffrey wanted,[16] but they were a marked advance over anything Crabbe had previously done in narrative. He mentions Jeffrey's advice in his preface, and goes on to remark that the "characters which seemed to be at my disposal were not such as would coalesce into one body, nor were of a nature to be commanded by one mind . . . but rather beings of whom might be formed groups and smaller societies. . . ."[17] Observe here that he considered himself as having certain characters at his "disposal," giving the impression that they came to him asking to be put on paper, and that it was these whom he formed into "groups and smaller societies." This may have been quite literally true. He writes, as we know, to Mrs. Leadbeater that he endeavored to paint his characters "as nearly as I could and dared," and that "there is not one of whom I had not in my mind the original."[18] We find in the journals reprinted by the son (who did not, unfortunately, print nearly enough of them) such laconic remarks as that dated July 10, 1817, "Maiden at a ball; I hope not mistress too,"[19] where we see an awareness of the contradiction between appearance and reality forcing itself upon his consciousness, and which gives some indication of his method of working. A further indication of his interest in the lives of real men is furnished by a letter to Sir Walter Scott, whose reference to himself as "fagging as a clerk" to the Supreme Court of Scotland draws the following reply from Crabbe:

. . . how the same hand that held the pen of Marmion, holds that which a clerk fags, unless a clerk means something vastly more than I understand—is not to be comprehended. I wait for elucidation, know you, dear sir, I have often thought I should love to read reports; that is, brief histories of extraordinary cases, with the judgments. If that is what is meant by reports, such reading must be pleasant; but, probably, I entertain wrong ideas, and could not

15 Jeffrey, *Contributions*, p. 321.

16 *Ibid.*, p. 322.

17 Ward, vol. II, p. 6.

18 *Life*, p. 221.

19 *Life*, p. 215.

understand the books I think so engaging. Yet I conclude there are histories of cases, and have often thought of consulting Hatchard whether he knows of such kind of reading, but hitherto I have rested in ignorance . . .[20]

This shows not only Crabbe's interest, but something of the quality of his interest in human affairs. So there is considerable evidence that the characters were all drawn from life, but there is very little evidence that the actual occurrences, the plots in which these characters move, had much relation to anything outside of what the poet was able to invent. Nor is it necessary to believe so, for the smaller societies, perhaps coming themselves from observation, naturally set the characters in motion.[21] The point to be made is that there were societies; their smallness may indicate a deficiency in Crabbe's ability to organize his material, but since "large societies" were clearly not his aim it is unfair to hold this against him. He accomplished what he set out to do, and it is by this accomplishment that he must be judged.

This interaction of character upon character does not find a prominent place in all the tales, but it is never entirely absent (as it was not entirely absent from the stories in *The Borough*), and those tales, such as "The Parting Hour," where it is most nearly absent are apt to seem either slightly sentimental or, as in the case of "The Struggles of Conscience," somewhat preachy.[22] At any rate, Crabbe is no longer a descriptive poet in the sense either of describing scenery or characters, for in these tales there is action—psychological action, if nothing more—as there has never been in his works before. Of this action his public in 1812 approved, buying five editions in two years.[23]

[20] A. L. Humphries, *Picadilly Bookman,* Memorials of the House of Hatchard, London, 1893, pp. 55–56.

[21] See *Huchon,* p. 371, who prefers to take a more literal view than I of the plots of some of the tales.

[22] It is interesting that the reviewer in *The Critical Review* rated the first of these as among the best and the other among the worst of the collection. See *Huchon,* p. 369.

[23] *Huchon,* p. 369, note 6. The 1814 edition is marked "Fifth edition," but may have been only the third. See Ward, vol. III, p. 557.

There was a place at this time for Crabbe both as a poet and as a writer of fiction. The novel, since the time of the Roger de Coverly papers, had risen to full flower, and by 1800 had withered. Maria Edgeworth's *Castle Rackrent* (1800) had begun a new development in fiction, but this was not immediately followed by imitations, and *Sense and Sensibility* did not appear, unnoticed, until 1811. Canon Ainger points out (p. 103) that the success of *The Parish Register* was largely that of a new adventure in the world of fiction, and this must have been even more true with respect to the *Tales,* for these provided a kind of fiction which neither the poems of Scott, nor the novels of the sentimentalists," nor the tired "gothicizers" were supplying. As fiction it must have had its roots in Fielding and Fanny Burney and very possibly Miss Edgeworth, and we feel a surprising similarity of viewpoint between Crabbe and Jane Austen (who is said to have remarked that she could fancy herself being Mrs. Crabbe[24]). Crabbe's combination of the technique of fiction of manners (such as we see clearly in VI, "The Frank Courtship") with that of realistic fiction in comfortable heroic couplets must have had an effect on popular taste which it is now difficult to assess, except by the large sales which the work enjoyed.

The most important thing about these *Tales* from our standpoint is the greatly increased complexity of the human relationships Crabbe presents, and the depth to which he penetrates in his probing for causation, or in probing the character within the limitations he himself sets. In *Tales* XVII, "Resentment," for example, he starts with the proposition that there are women like wax, easily molded and easily changed, and others who, like smelted iron, "the forms retain / But once impressed will never melt again." The heroine of the tale is of the latter variety, and Crabbe shows how, having been deceived by her husband, she becomes a virtual ogress, dispensing largess to the paupers of the town, but when he is impoverished denying him even creature comforts and finally bringing about his death.

24 Elizabeth Jenkins, *Jane Austen,* New York, 1949, p. 202. *Cf.* Broadley and Jerrold, p. 42.

Without the initial proposition the story seems monstrous; when the limitation imposed by the author is taken into account, it is no less credible than contemporary fiction founded on the theses of Freud.

But this story is somewhat unusual because Crabbe's characters do not commonly have such singleness either of purpose in themselves or of conception in the author's mind. Their actions and emotions are seldom referred to a single motive, but to many and complexly interrelated ones. We see, for example, Dinah in "Procrastination," *Tales* IV, who, when her Rupert returns after long absence (the basic theme is the Enoch Arden one), is very seriously torn between different ways of receiving him. Her avarice, her acquired fine manners finally win (and this is one of Crabbe's most withering themes), but we watch with fascinated dismay as the entire tale to that point is brought to bear upon the moment when she sends him away. W. C. Brown remarks that this tale "succeeds as narrative fiction because its people are never merely symbols of moral abstractions. Their world is not the black-and-white world of right and wrong: it is the actual world with infinite mixtures of the two, in which these people live as complex human beings."[25] Short of repeating the entire tale there is scarcely any way to demonstrate this, for "Procrastination" is one of Crabbe's narratives where there is no lost motion; every line has its place and its significance. This is true, as a matter of fact, of a larger proportion of the *Tales* than of any other of Crabbe's works.

In *Tales of the Hall,* which seems to me Crabbe's highest achievement, we are apt to feel that there is a certain amount of lost motion. It is a very long work (over 13,000 lines), and in many parts more slow-moving and reflective than anything Crabbe had previously written. It takes patience to read, and re-reading to understand, but the personality which emerges from the re-reading is worthy of anyone's acquaintance, and the form in which that personality has expressed itself is worth our observation. FitzGerald remarked that, "The Book, if I mistake not, deals rather with the follies than with the vices of man,

25 W. C. Brown, *The Triumph of Form*, p. 181.

with the comedy rather than the tragedy of life. Assuredly there is scarce anything of that brutal or sordid villainy of which one has more than enough in the Poet's earlier work. And even the more sombre subjects of the book are relieved by the colloquial intercourse of the narrators, which twines about every story, and, letting in occasional glimpses of the country round, encircles them all with something of dramatic unity and interest."[26] The colloquial intercourse of the two brothers is indeed important, forming as it does the framework into which the tales themselves are set.

The framework as a device was, in 1819, not at all unfamiliar to Crabbe, for he had made use of it in every previous work: it is obvious in *The Parish Register* and *The Borough* and appears in "The Widow's Tale," the seventh of the *Tales,* where the story within the frame is effectual in bringing about the conclusion of the frame story. Dr. Bär, in *George Crabbe als Epiker,* has made a very detailed and technical study of this aspect of Crabbe's writing, and I do not propose to repeat his labors; but we must notice that in *Tales of the Hall* and in that series of the *Posthumous Tales* united under the title "The Farewell and Return" Crabbe makes use of the framework, clearly, as a device by which he may remove himself at least one degree from the story he is presenting. This had been a continuing effort. As early as Part III of *The Parish Register* we find Old Dibble, the exemplary sexton, taking over the narrative from the omniscient author and telling his own story, and in Part I we have approaches to the dramatic form toward which Crabbe seemed constantly working.[27] In *The Borough* we have a number of instances of purely dramatic dialogue with no interposition of the author whatsoever,[28] and in almost all the *Tales* there are long sections composed entirely of the speeches of characters. These speeches are by no means always a rapid interchange of conversation, and are so much the less dramatic,

26 Edward FitzGerald, "Introduction" to "Readings in Crabbe," *Letters and Literary Remains,* London, 1903, vol. VII, p. 356.

27 See, for example, *Parish Register,* Part I, 563–575.

28 See, for example, Letter X, 149–168.

but Crabbe is at times capable of writing dialogue which could
be effectively staged:

> "Unhappy child! what labour will it cost
> "To win him back!"—"I do not think him lost."
> "Courts he then, trifler, insult and disdain?"—
> "No: but from these he courts me to refrain."—
> "Then hear me, Sybil: should Josiah leave
> "Thy father's house?"—"My father's child would grieve."—
> "That is of grace; and if he come again
> "To speak of love?"—"I might from grief refrain."—
> "Then wilt thou, daughter, our design embrace?"—
> "Can I resist it, if it be of grace?"—
> "Dear Child! in three plain words thy mind express—
> "Wilt thou have this good youth?"—"Dear father! yes."
>
> [*Tales* VI, 485–496.]

In a later tale we find a splendidly dramatic use of dialogue, the
simple tenderness of which is still effective:

> "Did he not curse me, child?"—"He never cursed,
> "But could not breathe, and said his heart would burst."
> "And so will mine."—"Then, father, you must pray;
> "My uncle said it took his pains away."
>
> [*Tales* XX, 391–394.]

Now Dr. Bär would deny that this dramatic tendency is related to any effort to achieve objectivity, and proposes, rather,
that it is an effort to avoid responsibility to his parishioners and
fellow-clergymen,[29] but, if only because it is a progressive
tendency which is most marked in the work which was least
likely to contain material offensive to the poet's contemporaries,
I feel free to decline accepting his theory. It seems to me quite
in accord with Crabbe's own disposition that he should be concerned with removing himself from his material, with attaining

---

29 Bär, p. 20: "Ich möchte vielmehr annehmen, dass Crabbe mit bewusster Rück-
sichtsnahme auf seinen Beruf als Geistlicher davon abgesehen hat, seine Standes-
genossen zu kritisieren, zumal da er sie vielleicht wie so viele Gestalten seiner
Dichtungen nach lebenden Vorbildern gezeichnet hat. Er überlässt deshalb . . .
die Erzählung und damit zugleich die Verantwortung für alles, was er uns zu
berichten hat."

greater objectivity not only through the frame-device itself, but also through the use of an explicitly dramatic form. One entire tale in *Tales of the Hall*, Book XIV, "The Natural Death of Love," is, after the introductory frame material, composed entirely in the form of a dialogue with tag-letters to differentiate the speakers, and while none of the other books in this work shows so clearly the poet's leanings toward complete objectivity (though we must remember "Flirtation—A Dialogue" which is dated May, 1816), it is essential to keep in mind that all of the narrative is at least once removed from the poet—that is, he is recording a tale told by one of the brothers or their friends—and sometimes as much as five times removed, as in lines 337 to 346 of "Ruth," Book V, where each line is preceded by four quotation marks.[30]

The framework itself constitutes an interesting story—we realize that it is a story of some scope when we consider that five of the twenty-two books are devoted to it—which concerns a pair of half-brothers who have not met since childhood. One is now the proprietor of the Hall, the other, poor and proud, has been invited to visit him at his estate. It is with reluctance that Richard accepts the invitation, just as it was with reserve, though with a lonely bachelor's need for friendship, that the invitation was extended. The brothers meet, tell one another their life stories, and then as they ride through the estate the association of ideas, their reflections upon or questions about the men and women whom they have met, lead them quite naturally to relate tales, the life histories of those whom they have encountered or of whom they are reminded. Meanwhile the brothers themselves are becoming better acquainted; they gradually reveal their characters to one another quite fully, but it takes time for George's reserve and Richard's pride to meet, and the moment when Richard first becomes really aware that his

---

[30] The complicated system of quotes within quotes was used by Crabbe himself in the original edition of *Tales of the Hall*, and has been retained in the Ward edition. Other editions, notably the Oxford Standard edited by A. J. and R. M. Carlyle, have not followed the original in this respect.

brother is as human as he, comes late in their story and assumes something of quiet drama. Richard speaks:

> "Then, thou too, Brother, couldst of weakness tell;
> "Thou, too, hast found the wishes that rebel
> "Against the sovereign reason; at some time
> "Thou hast been fond, heroic, and sublime . . .
>
> .   .   .   .
>
> "Then, be thy weakness to a Brother shown,
> "And give him comfort who displays his own."
>   "Ungenerous youth! dost thou presuming ask
> "A man so grave his failings to unmask?"
>
> [*Tales of the Hall* VII, 41–52.]

To me, at least, it is not at all clear why Huchon (p. 429) states that "Richard and George remain indistinct and unreal . . . They never take shape, they never become alive. The author describes them, but he does not see them and does not make us see them." If Huchon means that we do not visualize them in the way we can visualize Mr. Micawber I suppose we must agree; if he means that by the time we come to Book XXII we are not acquainted with the two men, I think we can feel free to dissent. In this final book we share with Richard the hesitations and doubts occasioned by his impending departure, but when it is suddenly revealed that George has equipped for Richard a farm on his estate and transported there Richard's wife, Matilda, and children, we just as suddenly realize that this is perfectly in accord with George's temperament, and that, faced with the *fait accompli*, Richard will accede to the pleasant arrangement.

Within this substantial framework, the tales are not always so artfully disposed as we might ideally prefer. Crabbe himself wrote to Murray, his publisher, that after the story of the elder brother, Book VII, the tales might follow in almost any succession they preferred;[31] but this apparent unconcern with the totality of the work, however much it may have been characteristic of Crabbe, is less disruptive of the unity of effect which the

31 *Huchon*, p. 405, note 3.

work achieves than we might suppose would be the case, for in every book the frame-story introduces the brothers, if only for a moment, engaged in the outwardly uneventful business of getting acquainted. We must not make too much of the fact that occasionally one of the stories is peculiarly suited to the character of the brother who happens to relate it (as is the case with Book XVIII, "Ellen"), but we cannot ignore that with the constant introduction of the brothers the frame-story does progress throughout the work, and we must admit the limitations of the plan Crabbe was employing. The frame Crabbe chose seems admirably adapted to his own temperament, showing as it does the two brothers in their reflective and analytical moods, and to what I take to be the real purpose for which he used a frame at all, that is, as another medium in addition to the dramatic tendency of the narratives themselves by which he could achieve the objectivity through which his understanding charity could best express itself.

> "How is it, men, when they in judgment sit
> "On the same fault, now censure now acquit?
> "Is it not thus, that *here* we view the sin,
> "And *there* the powerful cause that drew us in?
> " 'Tis not that men are to the evil blind,
> "But that a different object fills the mind.
> "In judging others we can see too well
> "Their grievous fall, but not how grieved they fell;
> "Judging ourselves, we to our minds recall,
> "Not how we fell, but how we grieved to fall."
>
> [*Tales of the Hall* III, 396–405.]

The poet who is seriously concerned with drawing those distinctions will also be concerned not to involve too deeply his personality in his work.

The obvious objection to this thesis is that Crabbe has involved himself very deeply in the characters of the two brothers. Many incidents in the early life of the younger brother, Richard, in particular, recall what must have been the youth of the poet himself. Richard says of himself as a boy, for example:

"I sought the town, and to the ocean gave
"My mind and thoughts, as restless as the wave;
"Where crowds assembled, I was sure to run,
"Hear[d] what was said, and mused on what was done;
"Attentive listening in the moving scene,
"And often wondering what the men could mean."

[*Tales of the Hall* IV, 295–300.]

This was very probably Crabbe's own experience, but he has made it Richard's. To say as does Huchon (p. 414) that his youth is identical with Crabbe's is to mistake the creative process, just as it would be a mistake to insist that the *Weltanschauung* of the older brother, George, is entirely Crabbe's own. Certainly the opening 130 lines of Book IV incorporate certain reflections of the elderly poet, but they are quite transmuted into those of the fictional character; I would say that these particular lines represent a debate of the poet with himself, he, meanwhile, in his own person, becoming engaged on neither side. There is no evidence that Crabbe was in any way so much involved with the characters of the two brothers that we must modify the thesis that his use of the frame-story was one of the ways in which he attempted to achieve objectivity.

In the *Posthumous Tales* we see very clear evidences of the same attempt. It is not entirely fair to make critical judgments upon the basis of these final works, for we know that they were left uncorrected and in many instances represent sketches rather than finished products. In the series entitled "The Farewell and Return," however, we note again the use of a framework. In this case, Crabbe is not so much concerned with tracing the development of a situation as in pointing out with great succinctness the ironical contrasts which are apparent to a man returning to his native place after an absence of twenty years. The "Poet" first tells of the impression a certain figure made upon him at the time he left his home, and then in a separate section he questions the "Friend," who brings the story up to date. The idea is one particularly useful to Crabbe, for it gives him an opportunity to present exactly those satirical, ironical aspects of life which often attracted him; but so far as the framework is concerned, he seems fairly early in the series to have found it cumbersome, and it is kept quite in the background, serving only as a device by which Crabbe lets the tale, or at least the dénouement, be told ostensibly through the eyes of another person. These final tales, even in their unfinished state, are entirely consistent with the development which we have seen in Crabbe's narrative work: the development from the mere narrative sketch to the full-blown psychological study, and the constant development in the direction of greater objectivity through the tendency toward dramatic writing and through the use of a narrative framework by which the poet might place himself at one remove from his material in order to survey it with the dispassion which was his goal.

3

It should be sufficiently obvious that although Crabbe sought to see and write dispassionately, he did not avoid the human passions as subject matter for his verse. What else, after all, is there about which to be dispassionate? Yet there are fashions in passion, just as there are fashions in everything else, and it is exceedingly difficult for an author to remain altogether uninfluenced by these. Crabbe was perhaps open to particular temptation, because he was primarily an author of fiction, and the kind of fiction he was interested in writing was, during his lifetime, in the center of one of these fashions.

Through all the later years of the eighteenth century wander fictional ladies and gentlemen who weep profusely, faint at slight provocation, and go into ecstasies at the merest glance from the opposite sex. This vogue was prevalent at the time Crabbe began to write, and continued unabated through the early years of the nineteenth century. There is every probability that the young and middle-aged poet was affected by these stories—the son records that Mrs. Inchbald's pathetic *Nature and Art* "almost broke our hearts"[32]—for he is able, on occasion, to employ their conventions when they suit his convenience.

[32] *Life*, p. 151.

But there is also no doubt that he was able to see through them, and he did not take their troubled heroes and heroines very seriously.[33]

This convention represents one aspect of the "romantic" temperament, and is one step in the development of the Shelleyan "romantic"—the young man who is aflame with ideals, who burns to reform the world, and who is constantly in the boil and bubble of some kind of emotional crisis. Crabbe knew and wrote of this temperament, but it is to him only one among other strange human phenomena which he observed with amused detachment. But Crabbe was well aware that this temperament could have serious manifestations, and these he was prepared to take seriously, as we can see in *Tales of the Hall* XX, "Smugglers and Poachers." Robert, one of the chief characters, is a Shelleyan "romantic":[34]

> The brothers met not often—when they met,
> James talk'd of honest gains and scorn of debt,
> Of virtuous labour, of a sober life,
> And what with credit would support a wife.
>   But Robert answer'd—"How can men advise
> "Who to a master let their tongue and eyes?
> "Whose words are not their own? whose foot and hand
> "Run at a nod, or act upon command?
> "Who cannot eat or drink, discourse or play,

---

[33] See *The Borough*, Letter XX, 11–119. These lines deal mostly with the "Gothic" fiction, but there are asides on the sentimentalists which are appropriate for our purposes. We must remember also that "Gothic" and "sentimental" fiction were by no means different genres, but had become thoroughly mixed by 1812. See lines 113–119:

> "Now, should we grant these beauties all endure
> Severest pangs, they've still the speediest cure,
> Before one charm be wither'd from the face,
> Except the bloom, which shall again have place,
> In wedlock ends each wish, in triumph all disgrace;
> And life to come we fairly may suppose
> One light, bright contrast to these wild dark woes."

[34] The family name of the two brothers, incidentally, is "Shelley," which is the only indication of which I am aware that Crabbe may have been familiar at all with the works of the poet Shelley.

"Without requesting others that they may.
"Debt you would shun; but what advice to give,
"Who owe your service every hour you live! . . ."

[*Tales of the Hall* XX, 74–85.]

Robert had very likely been reading Godwin or one of his disciples, but had he been aware of what happened in the third of Crabbe's *Tales,* "The Gentleman Farmer," he might have been less enthusiastic, for there the Godwinian gentleman farmer ends ironically under the complete subjugation of his steward, his physician, and his wife. The fate reserved for Robert is even more unpleasant—as a poacher he is shot by his brother, the gamekeeper—and between the two tales we are left in no doubt as to Crabbe's own opinion on such ideas.

The Godwinians seldom appear in his stories, but Crabbe does have a great many lovers in his tales, and these deserve special attention. About half of the *Tales* deal either with love or marriage, and the proportion in *Tales of the Hall* is slightly higher. We can easily deduce from his stories that Crabbe understood thoroughly the "theory," so to speak, of romantic love, but we know also as a sober fact related soberly by his son that he had experienced it in his own person; although it is hardly safe to deduce his biography from his writings, we can assume that he knew some of the disappointments and frustrations to which romantic love can lead. When we remember that his own marriage had been delayed for almost ten years, it need not surprise us to find him writing at least two tales showing the dangers of such delay;[35] but he was never embittered by the fact that this marriage, entered into after such painful waiting, ended in his wife's terrible, slow illness and eventual insanity. The little poem which the son found written on the paper in which his mother's wedding ring was wrapped is enough to prove that Crabbe never became cynical about love:

The ring so worn, as you behold,
So thin, so pale, is yet of gold.

[35] *Tales,* IV, "Procrastination," and *Tales of the Hall* XIII, "Delay has Danger."

> The passion such it was to prove:
> Worn with life's cares, love yet was love.
>
> [A. W. Ward ed., vol. III, p. 414.]

There is nothing either cynical or sentimental about these
verses, and when it suits his literary purposes, Crabbe can be
just as serious and manly about the loves of his characters. Ordinarily, however, he prefers to introduce us to them after the
love-pangs are already past and the long business of getting used
to one another has begun. With the ecstasies of love the poet
has usually not much sympathy, though he occasionally derives
some amusement from them.

I think we are apt to be deceived by Crabbe's handling of
lovers. George, for example, the elder brother and owner of the
Hall, has been a sentimental "romantic":

> "Turn with me to my twentieth year, for then
> "The lover's frenzy ruled the poet's pen;
> "When virgin reams were soil'd with lays of love,
> "The flinty hearts of fancied nymphs to move:
> "Then was I pleased in lonely ways to tread,
> "And muse on tragic tales of lovers dead;
> "For all the merit I could then descry
> "In man or woman was for love to die."
>
> [*Tales of the Hall* VII, 62–69.]

As we read the narrative of George's sentimental affair, we may
have an unpleasant feeling that Crabbe is letting himself be
ruled too much by the narrative conventions—perfectly honorable conventions, but not suited to the poet's temper. We forget, however, that Crabbe in his own person has said of George:

> George . . . rashly loved;
> Gave to a strong delusion all his youth,
> Led by a vision till alarm'd by truth.
>
> [*Tales of the Hall* I, 16–18.][36]

And if we feel uncomfortable in the presence of George's affair,
we must not forget that the poet has had George say in the preceding book:

[36] It is interesting to recall here the verse "To Mira" quoted in the first essay.

"O! my dear Richard, what a waste of time
"Gave I not thus to lunacy sublime . . ."

[*Tales of the Hall* VI, 340–341.]

In fact in the very book in which George tells his somewhat lugubrious adventures, we have this interchange between the brothers. Richard addresses George:

"Nay, spare me, Brother, an adorer spare:
"Love and the gout! thou wouldst not these compare?"
   "Yea, and correctly; teasing ere they come,
"They then confine their victim to his home:
"In both are previous feints and false attacks,
"Both place the grieving patient on their racks:
"They both are ours, with all they bring, for life,
" 'Tis not in us t'expell or gout or wife;
"On man a kind of dignity they shed,
"A sort of gloomy pomp about his bed;
"Then, if he leaves them, go where'er he will,
"They have a claim upon his body still;
"Nay when they quit him, as they sometimes do,
"What is there left t'enjoy or to pursue?"

[*Tales of the Hall* VII, 9–22.]

The implications of this for the sentimental married-and-lived-happily-ever-after formula are obvious. Crabbe does not even bother to be skeptical, for skepticism implies a doubt on both sides of the issue: if we are skeptical about the end of the world coming tomorrow, we grant the possibility that it may. Crabbe does not even grant the possibility that the formula as a formula has validity. He does not deny the existence of happy marriages by any means—we see Richard in *Tales of the Hall* as half of a perfect team, and in "Jesse and Colin" (*Tales* XIII) and the little portrait of Sir Edward Archer in the second part of *The Parish Register* we have similar fortunate marriages— but he goes against the fictional trend of his time, and indeed of ours, in denying that happiness is the inevitable concomitant of the nuptial ceremony.

There is little of sentimentalism in Crabbe—that is, as Professor Havens defines it, little of "tender emotion severed from action and indulged in for its own sake"[37]—and nothing of the belief that the happiness any more than the woes of men is the result of pure accident. There is no revelling in pity for its own sake, for none of Crabbe's characters are ever "put-upon" meaninglessly. If there is occasionally overstressed emotion, it is in the story for a fictional purpose, and is itself part of the point of the tale.[38] In only two of Crabbe's narratives, "The Parting Hour," *Tales* II, and "Ruth," *Tales of the Hall* V, is accident the deciding factor in the story, so in only two of his tales could there be a "sentimental" plot—and these, I think, are not sentimental. Nor is there exaggerated regret. Crabbe's characters occasionally indulge in it, but the poet then is very careful to stand off and to make his own position clear. We see this situation in the fourteenth of the *Tales of the Hall*, where the wife is loudly lamenting the passing of the first ecstatic bliss of marriage, while the husband realizes that they must make the best of what they have. It is important here, where the situation of regret becomes explicit, that Crabbe adopts the form of the dialogue to remove himself as far as possible from the matter he is presenting. The crucial passage is as follows (since it is all one speech by one of the characters, the dialogue form is not evident in the quotation):

> Lo! when the buds expand the leaves are green,
> Then the first opening of the flower is seen;
> Then comes the honied breath and rosy smile,
> That with their sweets the willing sense beguile;
> But, as we look, and love, and taste, and praise,
> And the fruit grows, the charming flower decays;
> Till all is gather'd, and the wintry blast
> Moans o'er the place of love and pleasure past.
> So 'tis with beauty,—such the opening grace
> And dawn of glory in the youthful face;
> Then are the charms unfolded to the sight,

---

[37] R. D. Havens, "Discontinuity in Literary Development: The Case of English Romanticism," *S.P.*, XLVII, No. 1 (January, 1950), p. 105.

[38] An excellent example of this is "Villars," *Posthumous Tales* V.

Then all is loveliness and all delight;
The nuptial tie succeeds, the genial hour,
And, lo! the falling off of beauty's flower;
So, through all nature is the progress made,—
The bud, the bloom, the fruit,—and then we fade.
    Then sigh no more,—we might as well retain
The year's gay prime as bid that love remain,
That fond, delusive, happy, transient spell,
That hides us from a world wherein we dwell,
And forms and fits us for that fairy ground,
Where charming dreams and gay conceits abound;
Till comes at length th'awakening strife and care,
That we, as tried and toiling men, must share . . .

  . . . .

Come my dear friend, and let us not refuse
The good we have, by grief for that we lose.

[*Tales of the Hall* XIV, 206–235.]

The passing of youth, the realization that dreams are only dreams and no more, the strife and care and toil impinging upon the new adult consciousness, have always been favorite themes of poets past the blush of adolescence. But no matter how much Crabbe in his own person may have been moved by these themes (and I think we need not hesitate to hear even in this detachment the authentic voice of the poet himself, admitting that what is lost has been good, but asserting that what remains is also good), he has in his poem objectified them and given them their living flesh by separating them from his own.

This particular story is one of the most complex studies of courtship and marriage with which I am familiar. Beginning with a petulant quarrel over who made what promise before marriage, the two characters progress first to despair that anything can be saved from their present disillusionment, then to the mature realization that:

As careful peasants, with incessant toil,
Bring earth to vines in bare and rocky soil,
And, as they raise with care each scanty heap,
Think of the purple clusters they shall reap:

> So those accretions to the mind we'll bring,
> Whence fond regard and just esteem will spring;
> Then, though we backward look with some regret
> On those first joys, we shall be happy yet.
>
> [*Tales of the Hall* XIV, 417–424.]

People have to work and suffer for their happiness; the world is a place where there is little to be enjoyed and much to be endured, and what there is to be enjoyed in marriage is the result of labor.

Now there is only one objection which might probably be raised against the proposition that Crabbe is not sentimental, and that is his occasional sentimentalizing of women. He seems even outside his poetry to have had an ideal of womanhood which remained singularly unattacked by his acute observation. In a letter to Elizabeth Charter, dated August 25, 1819, we have a glimpse of this for the only time in his informal writings:

We have a Crowd assembled in our Market Place Tonight, Mr. Astley [the Tory candidate opposing John Benett] is come to eat Venison and give away Beer and People draw his Carriage and prostrate themselves to their Temporary Idol. So would others or the same to their Idol's Rival. One's Mind is sick with the tumultuous assemblies of unthinking Men. Women I should say, if I can call these unsexed Creatures in our Streets, Women! No! it cannot be; I will not think some Beings whom I love and esteem are of the same Nature. Women! it cannot be.[39]

In 1815 or 1816 he seems actually to have become engaged to a young woman more than thirty years his junior, and she was only too willing to enter into the engagement.[40] He writes to Mrs. Leadbeater: "I have, though at considerable distances, six female friends, unknown to each other, but all dear, very dear to me. With men I do not much associate; not as deserting, and much less disliking, the male part of society, but as being unfit for it; not hardy nor grave, not knowing enough, nor sufficiently acquainted with the every-day concerns of men."[41] The last

---

[39] Broadley and Jerrold, p. 236.   [40] See *Huchon*, pp. 386–388.

[41] *Life*, p. 222. The letter is dated December 1, 1816.

statement is amazing enough coming from the author of *The Borough*! Miss Ridout, for a short time his prospective second wife, was no doubt among the six to whom Crabbe referred, as was Miss Charter. Exactly why this "January and May" affair did not work out is not clear—it was apparently due partly to some objections on the part of Miss Ridout's family, but perhaps even more to the fact that it *was* a January and May alliance, bearing certain affinities to one which he himself had described in the second part of *The Parish Register*. There was a flush of excitement followed by cold good sense. This is no doubt the situation to which the Biographer refers when he remarks that "on one occasion at least, my brother and myself looked with sincere pleasure to the prospect of seeing our father's happiness increased by a new alliance."[42]

In evaluating the quoted letter to Miss Charter, we must keep all this in mind, but we must also remember he was writing to a sentimental young lady, fond of novels, who liked to be flattered and whom he liked to flatter. The letter presents precisely the subtle kind of flattery which Crabbe would immediately have sensed as being attuned to his correspondent's tastes, and I do not know, therefore, that we need weight it heavily in considering the several ladies in his tales who pine away for love in a suspiciously sentimental fashion. Of these there are only two around whom a plot is built—Dorothea in *Tales* VIII, "The Mother," and "Ellen" of *Tales of the Hall* XVIII.

To rehearse their stories would not be particularly profitable. They both were disappointed in love, and they both seem, somehow, just to evaporate as a result. Now whether young women actually conducted themselves in this manner in the early nineteenth century I am at a loss to say. Certainly they did so in fiction, and that in itself might be sufficient excuse for Crabbe to have included several of them in his large roster of very diverse females. But I would also suggest that in a time when women had very much less freedom than they have today, when marriage was their only career, and when, if they had any social station, they were almost completely debarred from any activity

[42] *Life*, p. 214.

which could effectively soften a real and serious disappointment, it might not have been at all impossible for a neurotic young woman literally to have pined away for love. The findings of modern psychosomatic medicine might substantiate this thesis. If Crabbe had consistently dwelt on this kind of thing we might have more reason to be suspicious, but certainly the dreadful female in *Tales* XVII, "Resentment," more than balances Dorothea, and there is more than one strong-minded woman in *Tales of the Hall* to set opposite poor Ellen—the heroine of "The Maid's Story" for example. And the down-to-earth parson at least once slyly casts doubt on the claims of these love-lorn ladies to our attentions. He has one of them who survived her ordeal reflect:

"I wished to die—and grief, they say, will kill;
"But you perceive 'tis slowly, if it will.
"That I was wretched you may well believe—
"I judged it right, and was resolved to grieve."

[*Tales of the Hall* XX, 237–240.]

Since there may well be a realistic basis for the ladies who do pine away, I do not think that there is anything in Crabbe's treatment either of love or women which forces us in any essential respect to change the conception of him as unsentimental.

Crabbe was aware that love is only one of many passions, but I think he was too shrewd to have said that it has no great influence upon the sum of life; if it seems at first glance to have had too great an influence upon the sum of Crabbe's stories, we must remember that the marriage relationship, or the relationship of people about to be married, afforded Crabbe his most fruitful theme. It was an ideal one for his purposes, enabling him to analyze fully, in a limited situation which is nevertheless probably the most complicated into which two people can enter, the effects of minds one upon another.

4

Some of the specific techniques by which these involvements are expressed in Crabbe's poetic narratives are splendidly discussed by Mr. W. C. Brown in *The Triumph of Form* (pp. 173–177), and certain aspects of Crabbe's narrative technique are exhaustively treated by Dr. Bär, but it might prove illuminating for us to observe what apparatus is brought to bear by the poet in one of his mature tales. We find neither all his strengths nor all his weaknesses in any single one of his stories, but the reader of "Sir Owen Dale," *Tales of the Hall* XII, encounters a fair mixture of his virtues and defects. Of tales better than "Sir Owen Dale" there is an abundance; "Delay Has Danger," which immediately follows, is one of Crabbe's best, and Mr. Strang (p. 120) has called "Smugglers and Poachers" "[t]he greatest of all Crabbe's Tales." Both of these are concentrated and fluent in a way which "Sir Owen Dale" hardly approaches, and both of them contain passages of verse which nothing in the other tale can equal. Yet if "Sir Owen Dale" does not display Crabbe's greatest merits, it does nevertheless display merits, and these are the merits which the reader of almost any one of Crabbe's stories can discover. I shall give a very brief summary of the action of the tale, and then discuss some details.

The tale is told by a clerical friend of the brothers, who has been absent some time from their circle (we discover later in the frame-story that he has been sent as an emissary to Richard's wife). The explanation of his activities, he says, will involve an unpleasant story, but one of the brothers points out that men like to see other men tortured at prize-fights, so why not listen to sad tales?

> Thus urged, the worthy rector thought it meet
> Some moral truth, as preface, to repeat;
> Reflection serious—common-place, 'tis true;
> But he would act as he was wont to do,
> And bring his morals in his neighbour's view.
> "O! how the passions, insolent and strong,
> "Bear our weak minds their rapid course along;
> "Make us the madness of their will obey;
> "Then die, and leave us to our griefs a prey!"
>
> [*Tales of the Hall* XII, 58–66.]

We notice here, incidentally, that Crabbe is quite capable of taking an objective and somewhat humorous view of his own profession. The "moral" of the rector is, in fact, the theme of the story, and after stating it, the cleric proceeds with his relation.

Impartial observers had long felt that there were buried passions in Sir Owen, but these had remained dormant in his safely married state. At the age of forty, however, he finds himself a widower:

> That wife expired, and great the loss sustain'd,
> Though much distress he neither felt nor feign'd:
> He loved not warmly; but the sudden stroke
> Deeply and strongly on his habits broke.
>
> [110–113.]

He begins to seek society and acquire social graces,

> But much refinement, when it late arrives,
> May be the grace, not comfort, of our lives.
>
> [134–135.]

In this state, when unwonted passions are beginning to stir, he meets Camilla, carries on a flirtation with her, and believing he sees signs of encouragement, proposes marriage. She has only been amusing herself, however, and rejects his offer, which so humiliates Sir Owen, so deeply wounds his pride, that he vows to seek revenge.

Four years elapse, when his nephew, Morden, arrives for a visit. This nephew was valiant and poor, and owed everything to Sir Owen, who proposes now to use him as the instrument of his revenge upon Camilla. The plan is that Morden is to entice Camilla to love him, and then to leave her heartbroken as she had left his uncle. Morden is an honorable young man, and hesitates to accede to this unusual proposal, but considers the benefits which his uncle has bestowed upon him and finally enters into a solemn oath, at the insistence of Sir Owen, to carry out the plan. The two young people naturally fall in love at once.

The resulting dilemma seems incapable of solution. Morden will neither consent to leave Camilla nor break the oath to his uncle, who, although he really no longer cares very much, just as a matter of principle will not release Morden from the obligation:

> The uncle grieved; he even told the youth
> That he was sorry, and it seem'd a truth;
> But, though it vex'd it varied not his mind;
> He bound himself, and would his nephew bind.
> "I told him this, placed danger in his view,
> "Bade him be certain, bound him to be true;
> "And shall I now my purposes reject,
> "Because my warnings were of no effect?"
> Thus felt Sir Owen as a man whose cause
> Is very good—it had his own applause.
>
> [489–498.]

At this point there is a short bar across the page, and we begin a new episode. Sir Owen had a highly esteemed tenant named Ellis, whose history is briefly traced. Ellis had married a vicar's niece, Alicia,

> Who, though she freely ventured on the life,
> Could never fully be the farmer's wife.
>
> [511–512.]

The couple have three daughters, however, and seem happily married until Cecil arrives in the neighborhood to learn agriculture. This young man has tastes above those common in the circles in which he was forced to move, and soon finds a companion in Alicia; the companion becomes the lover:

> Of farming weary—for the guilty mind
> Can no resource in guiltless studies find—
> Left to himself, his mother all unknown,
> His titled father, loth the boy to own,
> Had him to decent expectations bred,
> A favour'd offspring of a lawless bed;
> And would he censure one who should pursue

The way he took? Alicia yet was new;
Her passion pleased him; he agreed on flight;
They fix'd the method, and they chose the night.

[611–620.]

Ellis, naturally, is in despair and rage, and vows revenge.

Here there is another short bar across the page, and we come
back to the story of Sir Owen, who has of course heard of Ellis'
misfortunes and now, several years later, seeks him out to learn
the progress of his revenge. When asked, Ellis is disturbed:

Sir Owen saw his tenant's troubled state,
But still he wish'd to know the offender's fate.
  "Know you they suffer, Ellis?"—Ellis knew;
" 'Tis well! 'tis just! but have they all their due?
"Have they in mind and body, head and heart,
"Sustained the pangs of their accursed part!"—
  "They have!"—" 'Tis well!"—"and wants enough to shake
"The firmest mind, the stoutest heart to break."—
  "But have you seen them in such misery dwell?"—
"In misery past description."—"That is well."
  "Alas! Sir Owen, it perhaps is just;
"Yet I began my purpose to distrust;
"For they to justice have discharged a debt
"That vengeance surely may her claim forget."—
  "Man, can you pity?"—
                    "As a man I feel
"Miseries like theirs."—

[680–695.]

Ellis then goes on to tell in great detail how he found his wife
and her lover living under the most miserable conditions, with
another child, the man ill and near death:

"Now the lost pair, whom better times had led
"To part disputing, shared their sorrow's bed;
"Their bed!—I shudder as I speak—and shared
"Scraps to their hunger by the hungry spared."—
  "Man! my good Ellis! can you sigh?"—"I can:
"In short, Sir Owen, I must feel as man . . ."

[730–735.]

There follows one of Crabbe's "Dutch" pictures, told in the words of Ellis, of the miseries the two endured, miseries which were sufficient to turn Ellis' desire for revenge into pity. Cecil was already so near death as to be past help, but Alicia he takes with him and establishes her in a sequestered cottage on his farm. This relation has so impressed Sir Owen that his own desire for revenge is extinguished, and he urges Morden and Camilla to enjoy their happiness.

Now immediately, from this summary, we can observe an awkwardness in handling the problem of the relationship between the two stories. This was one of the few times Crabbe chose to work with so complicated a problem of sequence, and his handling is inexpert. We must notice also the awkward introduction of the characters. Morden bursts upon us at line 255 with no warning whatsoever, and the same is true, of course, of Ellis, who is even separated by a typographical symbol from the rest of the tale. Crabbe seems also not to make full use of his opportunities for developing more clearly the relationship between Morden and Sir Owen, but then that was not his object in the story; and if we are apt to find that it takes Sir Owen somewhat longer than necessary to come to the point with Camilla, I think that in making this criticism we must consider the taste of the age, which enjoyed having its scenes drawn out in detail.

The awkward introduction of characters and the inexpert handling of sequence are Crabbe's greatest technical weaknesses as a story teller. They are real defects; and even though we may understand that the poet preferred to give us the characters one at a time and as he needed them, allowing us to observe each one carefully before going on to the next, and even though we may sense that usually the sequence, perfectly simple to understand, is not in itself very important for what he wanted to do, it is difficult not to lament those deficiencies which seem to demonstrate Crabbe's lack of mastery of two basic techniques of his art—a lack of mastery which would be almost fatal in the prose short story. Other defects in this particular tale are not so important. If we feel a certain moral *gaucherie* in Ellis' disposition of his wayward wife, I think we should keep in mind the quite different outcome of *Tales* XVI, "The Confidant," one of Crabbe's most honest and most pleasing tales, where the generous husband entirely forgives the trespasses of his spouse. Alicia had, after all, committed a sin unforgivable in 1819, and Ellis acts most generously from the standards of his class and time. Sir Owen's sudden "conversion" to generosity at the end provides the necessary resolution; though it is actually much better prepared than I was able to indicate in the summary, it does come, perhaps, as too much of a surprise. Crabbe's plots are usually more organically developed.

I made it a point, in re-telling the story, to quote several passages, and these illustrate some of the virtues of Crabbe's technique. The practice of giving the theme of the tale in opening remarks is a very frequent one. In the *Tales* it appears usually in the first fifteen or twenty lines, and frequently in the very opening verses (as in *Tales* II and IV). This is helpful in orienting the reader in the situation into which he is immediately thrust, for Crabbe ordinarily gets on with the story very quickly. In four lines not quoted (81–84) we see the author foreshadowing not necessarily the outcome, but the critical action of the story. This also is a technique which Crabbe frequently employs with great skill.[43] His greatest strength, however, as demonstrated in this tale, is the manner in which he is able to carry forward the story by the use of narrative epigrams and dialogue.

Handled as fluently as Crabbe can use it at his best, the pentameter couplet seems to have distinct advantages as a narrative medium. Far from obstructing the invention of the author, it seems rather, by its very nature, to lend great emphasis to details which in a prose composition would require paragraphs to be given the same effect. In the lines

> "Man! my good Ellis! can you sigh?"—"I can:
> "In short, Sir Owen, I must feel as man . . ."

---

[43] See *The Borough* XIX, 118–121; *Tales* XX, 29–34; XIII, 107–108; XI, 261; XV, 92; XVI, 418–419; XXI, 330 ff.; *Tales of the Hall* VIII, 257–258, 289–290, 314; XII, 511–512; *Posthumous Tales* V, 95–96, 203; XVII, 258–259; XIX, 185.

I cannot but believe that the rhyme of *can* : *man* is intentionally inserted to focus attention on the latter word. Remember that Ellis has already said, "As a man I feel . . ." and the reappearance of the slightly altered phrase with the emphasis this time on "man" can hardly be accidental, pointing up, as it does, the inhumane, the unmanly feelings of Sir Owen which it is the purpose of the narration to reverse. In the same way there is a great concentration in the lines

> But much refinement, when it late arrives,
> May be the grace, not comfort, of our lives.

These convey essential information fully, briefly, and in a way far more calculated to strike the reader's attention than would a paragraph of prose. We can find these narrative epigrams in every one of Crabbe's stories, and this is the reason why we seem to know so much about what goes on in the world of his characters, why they are able to accomplish such an amount of meditation in the small space they are given, and why it is almost impossible to summarize one of Crabbe's stories without quoting. In the midst of a discursive passage we suddenly come upon the tiny grain which crystallizes the sense.

These rhetorical grains are not infrequently cast in surprisingly elegant language, but to complain that Crabbe's characters do not speak "naturally" is to judge by a standard which has no relevance. His son writes that "he had neither the turn, nor much of the talent for the retention of conversations; and even what he did remember, he was not always disposed to communicate. One maxim of Johnson's however, had made a strong impression on him: 'Never fear of putting the strongest and best things you can think of into the mouth of your speaker, whatever may be his condition.' "[44] This maxim represented one of the standards of the age, and the fact that Crabbe did not deviate from it is scarcely a fair basis for an adverse judgment. Sometimes, to be sure, Johnson's admonition seems stretched almost to the breaking point, as in the following melodramatic gem:

[44] *Life,* pp. 95–96.

> "Oh, miserable lot!"
> Exclaim'd the man; "Go, serpent! nor remain
> "To sharpen wo by insult and disdain . . ."
>
> [*Tales* XII, 277–279.]

But there are also passages where there is effective simplicity and appropriateness, as in this, spoken by the mother of "Ruth":

> " 'There were no lights without, and my good man,
> " 'To kindness frighten'd, with a groan began
> " 'To talk of Ruth, and pray; and then he took
> " 'The Bible down, and read the holy book;
> " 'For he had learning; and when that was done
> " 'We sat in silence—whither could we run? . . ."
>
> [*Tales of the Hall* V, 426–431.]

The genuine naturalness here in no way violates Johnson's precept, and even though no attempt is made to reproduce dialect, there is nothing which offends my conception, at least, of what the pious wife of a fisherman might have said. Certainly this naturalness is on the whole more characteristic of his passages of dialogue than is the melodramatic awkwardness.

Such awkwardness as Crabbe does display in his stories—and we can be very annoyed at his occasional clumsiness—is almost always in his handling of the details of plotting, as I have pointed out, or sometimes in the language itself, but almost never in the conception and manipulation of character. Of human psychology he had a most secure grasp, and one of the chief ways in which Crabbe's fiction, as fiction, differs from so much of that surrounding him is that his characters so often act particularly and understandably human. Paul Elmer More says of this "unerring psychological instinct" that it "is not confined to any one tale; it guides the poet in the creation of all his multitudinous characters. At first, perhaps, we see the ethical motives that underlie a character so clearly defined, it seems the poet is dealing with a moral type; but suddenly some little limitation is thrown in, some modification of motive, which changes the character from a cold abstraction to a living and unmistakable personality."[45]

We see an excellent example of this in the quoted passage concerning Cecil. Cecil up to this point has seemed merely a foppish philanderer, but suddenly there is the backward glance at his situation in the world—not condemning, not commiserating, simply showing us with true satiric balance things as they are—and at once his character takes understandable shape. At one stroke it becomes obvious why he is what he is. This, I should say, is the triumph of Crabbe's realism, for in this all the major attributes of Crabbe which we have previously discussed come together: his attention to outward circumstances, his ability to grasp a situation as it presents itself to him, but above all his charity, for a man who is not charitable will hardly bother so deeply to understand the creatures of whom he writes.

This also tends to contradict those who write of Crabbe as primarily a didactic author.[46] He does, very occasionally, wear his cassock while he writes,[47] and he not infrequently points up the "somewhat negative virtues," as Mr. Spingarn calls them, of common sense, obedience, and patience (although we should note the posthumous tale, "Barnaby the Shopman," where it becomes evident that Crabbe considered these commercial virtues insufficient unless informed by a more solidly Christian morality); but a man who has taken so much trouble to understand his characters is very likely more interested in the characters themselves than in what they can teach. Crabbe's son remarks that whereas the early works were didactic, in *The Parish Register* and those following "no moral inference is directly inculcated,"[48] and the poet himself, in his preface to *Tales of the Hall*, states flatly, in the very best neo-classic manner, that "The first intention of the poet must be to please . . ."[49] This great interest in his characters is no doubt also the reason

45 More, "Genius of Crabbe," p. 140.

46 For example Ainger, pp. 91–146; *Huchon* pp. 316–373, 403–431.

47 See *Tales of the Hall* XVI, 963 ff.; XVII, 530 ff.

48 *Life,* p. 176.   49 Ward, vol. II, p. 300.

why Crabbe tells the same story over again several times—but with significant differences. The parallel between "William Bailey" (*Tales of the Hall* XIX) and "Delay has Danger" (*Tales of the Hall* XIII) would be interesting to pursue in detail, as would the parallels in story between "The Will" (*Posthumous Tales* XX) and "The Cousins" (*Posthumous Tales* XXI); "The Parting Hour" (*Tales* II) and "Procrastination" (*Tales* IV) both employ the Enoch Arden theme, and there are other examples which might be cited. In all these cases the basic plot elements are the same, which might be taken as an example of Crabbe's infertility of invention but which, as I believe we can see after reading them, shows more pertinently that his chief interest is in character. The persons set into these plots are very different indeed. We can even believe that Crabbe purposely took the same themes over again (note that each of the cited pairs falls within a single published work) just because he was amused by manipulating his people.

It was the people of the world which interested Crabbe. Almost from his earliest composition he had directed his detached but searching mind toward the investigation of individual human beings, asking about them, watching them, writing about them. His abilities as a story-teller are not remarkable. He is not, as Mr. Forster points out, a novelist who missed his vocation, nor is he merely a short-story writer who happened to write in verse, even though he did in many ways anticipate by a century the "slice of life" school of fiction, and though he does have the merit, not common in his time, of allowing his best stories to develop organically without intruding his own person. But he does understand humanity, and he can make his reader understand; for although in order to clear away the technical underbrush of story-telling he may wield a machete, when the physician gets through the jungle to his patient, he is able to use the most delicate scalpel, and tenderly to lay bare the most intimate reaches of the human psyche. We may wish for various perfections which Crabbe did not attain, but, unique as he is, some may be happy in those which he possessed.

5 | CRITICISM
AND A CRITIQUE

Cʀɪᴛɪᴄꜱ have never been quite content with Crabbe, and generally for good reasons. He is not an easy author to label, as Mr. E. M. Forster has pointed out,[1] and, lacking the first-aid of a meaningful epithet, most critics have been content either to seize upon only one aspect of his work and to praise or condemn him for that alone, or else they have been forced by the multitude of contradictions which careful reading of his poetry reveals to relegate him to that poetic limbo the entrance to which is bordered by a frieze of "whereas's" and "on the other hand's." Yet, though this be almost the rôle of critiques of Crabbe, there is something to be learned by examining in more detail the fluctuations of opinion regarding his work.

Probably a fair portion of the popular approval of Crabbe during the later years of his life is accounted for in a letter to the poet written by Mrs. Leadbeater. She asks that he "Just give me leave to thank thee for giving us poetry which we may put into the hands of our children, without fear of their imbibing false ideas from the perusal of it, and also without fear of their

[1] Introduction to *Life*, p. xv. For an excellent summary of criticism see Walter E. Broman, "Factors in Crabbe's Eminence in the Early Nineteenth Century," *Modern Philology*, LI (August, 1953), pp. 42–49.

throwing it aside, as they might what was only didactic, and not given in narratives at once so true and so interesting . . . where sin is shewn to be exceedingly sinful, and its wages to be death. Oh! go on and prosper, for this is a good work!"[2]

Crabbe's answer to this letter is evasive; we have already seen that although he considered himself a moral poet, he did not have overtly didactic aims, but although none of the important contemporary criticism of his works tends to stress so strongly as Mrs. Leadbeater the inculcation of virtue, there is probably good reason to believe that some, at least, of his popularity is to be accounted for on that basis.

On the whole, Crabbe found favor with the early nineteenth-century critics, just as he did with the public. We have already observed that the "Lakists" looked upon him with some doubt, and, as might be expected, he failed to please Keats,[3] but according to Byron, "Crabbe's the man, though he has a coarse and impractical subject."[4] In this statement Byron hit the key-note for a great deal of contemporary opinion, for though perhaps only Jeffrey would have said "Crabbe's the man," certainly Lockhart and Gifford would have agreed with Byron as to his subject, and all three would have agreed with Leigh Hunt that:

Mr. Crabbe is unquestionably a man of genius, possessing imagination, observation, originality: he has even powers of the pathetic and terrible, but with all these fine elements of poetry, is singularly deficient in taste, his familiarity continually bordering on the vulgar, and his seriousness on the morbid and shocking.[5]

Lockhart was possibly somewhat less disturbed by the morbid and shocking elements in Crabbe's work than was Leigh Hunt, who, we should remember, wrote before *Tales of the Hall* had been published. "The national taste," he wrote,

---

[2] *The Leadbeater Papers*, vol. II, p. 352.

[3] Keats' offhand statement that he "liketh none of Crabbe" is to be found in *Letters*, ed. M. B. Forman, Oxford, 1931, vol. II, p. 352.

[4] *Works of Lord Byron:* "Letters and Journals," ed. R. E. Prothero, London, 1904, vol. IV, p. 169.

[5] Leigh Hunt, *The Feast of the Poets*, London, 1815, p. 46.

is, on the whole, a manly one; it is felt that life is made up of light and shadow in pretty equal proportions—and the only art that can permanently fix and please us, is that which has scope enough to reflect life in its own contrasts. Crabbe's deep, and sometimes dreadful pathos, tells on us a thousand times more than it would otherwise have done, by reason of the wit, the humour, the playful humanity with which he relieves it . . .[6]

Lockhart and FitzGerald make the only mention in the highly-serious nineteenth century of Crabbe's humor, one of his outstanding qualities, and the one which makes it possible to enjoy even those more depressing parts of *The Borough* which, in his enthusiasm for Crabbe, Jeffrey tried so hard to explain away.[7] Jeffrey was Crabbe's greatest critical friend, and when in 1846 he collected his essays from the *Edinburgh,* he remarks:

I have given a larger space to Crabbe in this republication than to any of his contemporary poets; not merely because I think more highly of him than most of them, but also because I fancy that he has had less justice done him. The nature of his subjects was not such as to attract either imitators or admirers, from among the ambitious or fanciful lovers of poetry; or, consequently to set him at the head of a School, or let him surround himself with the zealots of a Sect: And it must also be admitted, that his claims to distinction depend fully as much on his great powers of observation, his skill in touching the deeper sympathies of our nature, and his power of inculcating, by their means the most impressive lessons of humanity, as on any fine play of fancy, or grace and beauty in his delineations. . .[8]

In this criticism Jeffrey was in the center of most of the favorable nineteenth-century opinion of Crabbe. With him Gifford agreed, although with more reservations, holding as he did that poetry should take us out of the world "away from the fatigues of reality."[9] Had Gifford been less favorable, it is perfectly possible that Hazlitt would have been less testy in his

6 *Quarterly Review,* vol. L (1834), p. 469.

7 *Edinburgh Review,* vol. XX (1812), pp. 277 ff.

8 Jeffrey, *Contributions,* p. 274 n.

9 *Quarterly Review,* vol. IV (1810), p. 284.

amazing essay on "Mr. Campbell and Mr. Crabbe," where he carries the possible objections to Crabbe's poetry to an impossible extreme:

He takes the most trite, the most gross and obvious and revolting of nature, for the subject of his elaborate descriptions; but it is Nature still, and Nature is a great and mighty Goddess! . . . His Muse is not one of *the Daughters of Memory*, but the old toothless, mumbling dame herself, doling out the gossip and scandal of the neighbourhood. . . . Mr. Crabbe's Helicon is choked up with weeds and corruption; it reflects no light from heaven, it emits no cheerful sound; no flowers of love, or hope or joy spring up near it, or they bloom only to wither in a moment.[10]

Of Hazlitt's criticism Mr. S. J. Looker remarks:

It is a hard thing to say, but not unjust in the circumstances, that several of Crabbe's hostile critics read as if they had not studied his poetry with deep attention. Hazlitt is an outstanding example in his *Spirit of the Age*, in which he says he has read the Tales and that "they turn, one and all, upon the same sort of teazing, helpless, mechanical unimaginative distress." An opinion which is so unreasonable and so wide of the mark that it can be explained by no other supposition than that so acute a critic as Hazlitt usually shows himself to be, in this case had not read his author with any great care. It is probable that the great weight of Hazlitt's name has unduly affected the appreciation of the poet.[11]

Strang says of Hazlitt's criticism that it is "so utterly vicious that it is inexplicable except by the critic's prejudice and the carelessness which is its natural consequence."[12] Whether or not Hazlitt had read Crabbe carefully, it is important that in this criticism is first publicly levelled the "no poet" accusation which the later nineteenth century, under the spell of the magnificent lyrical outburst which occurred at the moment when Crabbe was completing his finest work, took up with vigor. Crabbe represented an opposite pole to that of the lyricism; he

10 "The Spirit of the Age," *Works*, ed. P. P. Howe, vol. XI, p. 164.

11 "In Praise of Crabbe," *Nineteenth Century and After*, October, 1931, p. 502.

12 Strang, *Crabbe*, p. 2.

represented, if we will, the factuality, the science of the preceding century, and it is evidently with this that Hazlitt, whether consciously or not, identifies him. Hazlitt's objection to the progress of scientific knowledge in his essay "On Poetry in General" is well known, and Miss Schneider points out that he was never able to reconcile his conception of art as escape, on one hand, and his belief that it should represent knowledge or truth, on the other.[13] This was one of the dilemmas of nineteenth-century criticism, and Crabbe inevitably fell foul of those who preferred to think of art as escape, and who felt that the intrusion of mere fact into poetry was, *ipso facto,* unpoetical.

The later nineteenth century felt also that it had become more conscious of technique, and those critics who were sympathetic with Crabbe obliged themselves to point out that in his own time he was not judged so harshly on this score as in theirs. In 1882 FitzGerald wrote, "Nevertheless, with all my own partiality for this book [*Tales of the Hall*], I must acknowledge that, while it shares with the Poet's other works in his characteristic disregard of form and diction—of all indeed that is now called 'Art'—it is yet more chargeable with diffuseness . . ."[14] Canon Ainger says of the story of Phoebe Dawson, "The Picture presented is as poignantly pathetic as Frederick Walker's *Lost Path* or Langhorne's 'Child of misery, baptized in tears.' That it will ever again be ranked with such may be doubtful, for *technique* is the first quality demanded of an artist in our day, and Crabbe's *technique* is too often defective in the extreme." (*Crabbe,* p. 99.) It was, indeed, the matter of technique which occasioned most of the unfavorable remarks bestowed upon Crabbe by two of the giants of late nineteenth-century criticism, Saintsbury and Leslie Stephen.

The latter is somewhat more kind to Crabbe, whose rough style, he says, "is indicative of his general temper. It is in places at least the most slovenly and slipshod that was ever adopted by

13 Elizabeth Schneider, *The Aesthetics of William Hazlitt,* Philadelphia, 1933, p. 115.

14 FitzGerald, "Introduction" to "Readings . . . ," ed. cit., p. 359.

any true poet."[15] Stephen laments that there are no great out-
bursts of poetic (lyric?) passion in his works, and, like Gifford,
tends to think that the details Crabbe selects are too "low" to
please, but he concludes his essay on a generally favorable note:

True, he does not appeal to emotions, accessible only through the
finer intellectual perceptions, or to the thoughts which "lie too deep
for tears." That prerogative belongs to men of more intense character, greater philosophical power, and more delicate instincts. But
the power of touching readers by downright pictures of homespun
griefs and sufferings is one which, to my mind, implies some poetical
capacity, and which clearly belongs to Crabbe.[16]

When, however, Stephen remarks that, "If Pope's brilliance of
style savours too much of affectation, Crabbe never manages to
hit off an epigram in the whole of his poetry" (p. 261), we can
only say with FitzGerald that there is ". . . many a shrewd remark so tersely put that I should call them epigrams did not
Mr. Stephen think the Poet incapable of such. . . ."[17] And we
may perhaps wonder how long it had been since Stephen had
read his author.

Following Professor Woodberry,[18] Saintsbury raises the question of whether or not Crabbe is at all a poet, and he concludes
that Crabbe is not, because, he says,

there is no wing in Crabbe, there is no transport, because, as I hold
(and this is where I go beyond Hazlitt), there is no music. In all
poetry, the very highest as well as the very lowest that is still poetry,
there is something which transports, and that something in my
view is always the music of the verse, of the words, of the cadence,
of the rhythm, of the sounds superadded to the meaning.[19]

Saintsbury does, however, find virtues in Crabbe—much the
same virtues of sympathetic humanity that Stephen and Jeffrey
found—"Therefore," he says,

[15] Leslie Stephen, *Hours in a Library*, London, 1876, vol. II, p. 259.

[16] *Ibid.*, pp. 288–289.

[17] FitzGerald, *op. cit.*, p. 359.

[18] Woodberry, "A Neglected Poet," *Studies* . . . , p. 44.

[19] Saintsbury, "Crabbe," *Essays* . . . , p. 26.

I shall conclude that save at the rarest moments, moments of some sudden gust of emotion, some happy accident, some special grace of the Muses to reward long and blameless toil in their service, Crabbe was not a poet. But I have not the least intention of denying that he was great, and all but of the greatest among English writers (p. 32.).

This was, in general, the view taken by Huchon, whose biographical treatment of Crabbe remains standard, but whose critical standard is that the less a poet is like Shelley the less he is a poet; he finds Crabbe generally unpoetical:

He became but was not born a poet. His sensibility, although lively and fairly keen, is not vibrant; his senses are far from having the subtle penetration of Shelley's. His austere temperament, in youth and middle age at least, lacks the softness, the richness, of those happy and slightly voluptuous minds from which poetry gushes forth without effort ... Too uniformly reasonable and calm, Crabbe becomes animated only on rare occasions and emits only transient gleams. Besides, he is hampered by the prosaic nature of his favourite subjects.[20]

Of Huchon's critical approach Mr. Strang in 1913 remarked:

M. Huchon, for example ... can see no other elements in Crabbe's realism than 'description, satire, pessimism.' I do not blame: I merely marvel at his perseverance in reading through the works of Crabbe, and pity him for his misfortune in missing so much of the humour. . . . To the grand qualities of the poet he is consistently fair, as most people are. The lighter note which comes in a multitude of variations at all sorts of places is neglected by him as by all except FitzGerald and the author of the "Theatre" in "Rejected Addresses." It is this, above all things, that lifts Crabbe out of the quicksands and miry clay.[21]

Since I have made use of it in earlier chapters, I shall not quote here from the essay by Paul Elmer More. So far as it applies to Crabbe's humor, Strang's remark applies almost equally to More's essay, but the latter, as might be expected, shows more respect for Crabbe as a poet than does Huchon.

20 *Huchon*, pp. 478–479.   21 Strang, *Crabbe*, pp. 73–74.

This is, in general, the trend of most twentieth-century writing on Crabbe, largely, I think, because only those who like Crabbe as a poet have bothered to publish their observations. E. A. Robinson's sonnet, "Crabbe" ("Give him the darkest inch your shelf allows") is a noteworthy tribute, and more recently F. L. Lucas,[22] and F. R. Leavis[23] have, each after his own manner, praised the poet, the former citing the clearness of Crabbe's vision, the latter his moving narrative as worthy of special remark.

This epitome of critical comment has obviously made no pretense to being exhaustive, but it must have indicated, as is true of more than one eighteenth-century author, that the fluctuations of opinion as to Crabbe's value as a poet interestingly reflect the changes in literary temper during the years since his death—a point which I should think would hardly need demonstration. The survey of opinion on Crabbe, however, should make evident some of the difficulties standing in the way of a fresh evaluation, for, with the exception of a very few obviously biased critics, who, like Hazlitt, denigrate him too much, or perhaps like Jeffrey exalt him too high, almost everything critics have said about Crabbe is true. That is the great difficulty; almost everything one can say about the poetry, there is something in that poetry to refute. We may today be less concerned than was Saintsbury with the quality of "transport" in poetry, and Crabbe himself would have been sorely puzzled at the thought of even looking for it in his verse; yet there are moments, if I understand the quality, when it can be detected. On the other hand if we are content to say that Crabbe's handling of his meter was only thoroughly adequate, there are passages which seem to place even this modest proposition in doubt. Since so much ink has already been spent on the question of Crabbe's verse, the expenditure of a little more need not be grudged. And the question itself is more interesting than would at first be supposed.

[22] F. L. Lucas, "The Poet of Prose," *Life and Letters*, vol. VI (1931), pp. 79–105.

[23] F. R. Leavis, *Revaluation* . . . , New York, 1947, pp. 124–129.

2

Enough of his best verse has already been quoted in the course of this study to convince anyone, I believe, but the most adamant enemy of the heroic couplet that Crabbe was capable of writing poetry at least of first-rate quality, even if not poetry which ascends the highest pinnacles of greatness.[24] First-rate poetry is not so frequently found that we can afford to ignore its maker. If some readers still so fear the "rocking horse" as to deny that the heroic couplet is a possible medium for poetry, those I must leave behind in the following discussion, the purpose of which is less to praise Crabbe's good verse, which needs no defense, than to accord due acknowledgment to certain merits in parts of his work where the faults are more conspicuous.

It is interesting that Stephen, in quoting "bad lines," selects in every case the opening lines of a story. Perhaps he was discouraged by an inauspicious beginning from proceeding further, but I suspect that, in search of bad lines, Stephen simply went where bad lines are most easily to be found. Now Crabbe's narrative intent forced upon him the problem of conveying immediately enough information to enable the reader to pick up the story line quickly and intelligently; but this problem of conveying information—of a necessarily commonplace sort when the tale is to deal with every-day material—is not one which has been peculiar to Crabbe. We cannot justify one poet's prosiness by quoting the prosaic lines of another, but we may remind ourselves that other poets, faced with this problem of conveying information in the opening lines of a story, have often been hampered by the same difficulties. It seems slightly unfair to charge Crabbe with defects that on closer scrutiny appear inherently characteristic of the genre in which he worked.

> Counter and Clubb were men in trade, whose pains,
> Credit, and prudence, brought them constant gains.
>
> [*Tales* XVIII, 1–2.]

[24] See, for example, *The Borough* IX, 173–205; XXII, 181–204; *Tales of the Hall* XIII, 701–724; XIV, 206–235. All these have been quoted at various points in these essays.

These are not very good lines; by themselves they are about as prosaic as any Crabbe wrote, but, as Leslie Stephen failed to point out when he quoted them, they serve their function in the story as a whole. So do these lines:

> A marchant whilom dwelled at Seint Denys
> That riche was, for which men helde hym wys.
>
> [*The Shipman's Tale*, 1–2.]

And these:

> These tourists, heaven preserve us! needs must live
> A profitable life: some glance along,
> Rapid and gay . . .
>
> [Wordsworth, *The Brothers*, 1–3.]

And these more famous verses:

> If from the public way your turn your steps
> Up the tumultuous brook of Green-head Ghyll . . .
>
> [*Michael*, 1–2.]

If Saintsbury's "transport" is to be the criterion for verses snatched out of context, I am not entirely sure that Chaucer or Wordsworth, in the quoted instances, have met it more successfully. Some readers are uninterested in trade, while others may be uninterested in brooks, even if tumultuous; one reader will, therefore, find immediately that one poem interests him more than the other. Nor will readers uninterested in the bucolic life be encouraged by however fine a poem beginning:

> With farmer Allan at the farm abode
> William and Dora. William was his son;
>
> [Tennyson, *Dora*, 1–2.]

Tennyson is able, perhaps, to make his opening lines convey more necessary information than did Wordsworth, but I think his verses, although smoother, are on about the same level of "transport" as Crabbe's. All three poets were struggling with a problem indigenous to the genre in which they were working.

Now this is not to make any generalizations about the verse tale as such, and indeed, generalizations about the verse tale of common life would have to be based largely on the work of Crabbe, but I think it should somewhat soften condemnation of Crabbe's opening couplets. He shows a marked preference for getting his incidental matter out of the way as quickly as possible, and his opening lines, just as do the opening lines of stories by Wordsworth and Tennyson, serve this purpose. Similarly, we must beware of picking passages simply at random and condemning the poetry as bad. Narrative poetry, unlike lyric, deals with a *succession* of events or moods, and the poet must contrive some way of proceeding from one, perhaps lyrical, point in his story to another. The standard of judgment, then, in the cases of a lyric and a narrative poem, must be somewhat different, for when we consider the necessary bridgework of a tale, we hardly have any reason to expect that we are to be kept constantly on the wing. Here is a prosaic and awkward passage picked from the middle of one of Crabbe's tales:

> Again returned, the matron and the niece
> Found the late quiet gave their joy increase;
> The aunt, infirm, no more her visits paid,
> But still with her sojourn'd the favourite maid.

> [*Tales* VI, 137–140.]

There is a great deal of necessary information packed into these lines, and although there are ungraceful inversions in the final couplet, the worst that can be said of the passage is that it is mediocre. It is in no way a deviation from the heroic-couplet convention with which Crabbe's readers were intimately familiar, and I do not believe we need expect that the passage do more than take us from one point to another, while conforming in pattern to the rest of the poem. At the very least, we may be grateful that Crabbe did not attempt to dress up his rhetorical hinges with high-sounding bombast. If the information that an old maid has ceased to pay her visits would not ordinarily excite our more delicate poetic sensibilities, there is no reason to expect it to do so here, where, though it is in verse, no particular poetic claims are made for it.

As a matter of fact, Stephen made a somewhat unfortunate

choice when he quoted the Counter and Clubb couplet as an example of the nadir of Crabbe's verse. It is generous to assume that he had read the rest of the tale which the lines introduce, for certainly he made no effort to fit the lines into a context. The couplet forms the introduction to a satiric and humorously ironic retelling of the classic tale of two merchants, Counter and Clubb (and should not the names themselves disclose something of the tone of the story?), who disagree about the kind of woman who makes the best wife. Clubb marries a strong-willed woman to whom he submits, and for this reason must endure the scorn of Counter, whose wife, a "clinging vine," is apparently under his domination. A wager, however, proves Clubb to have the more reasonable spouse, a woman who actually grants him more freedom than Counter's, who exercises the omnipotent tyranny of tears. The opening couplet forecasts in tone the whole story, and has besides the merit of contributing its share of the necessary background.

We could similarly examine other "bad" opening lines, and others of those necessary passages which serve to keep a story in motion and have no other purpose. We should probably not find them all so defensible as the Counter and Clubb lines, but they would invariably gain by being placed in context. Even the lines, berated by Leslie Stephen,

> With our late Vicar, and his age the same,
> His clerk, hight Jachin, to his office came.
>
> [*The Borough* XIX, 1–2.]

which admittedly display almost every one of Crabbe's faults as a maker of verses, are quickly forgiven as the reader moves into one of Crabbe's most powerful stories. They are forgiven because, seen in the light of the entire tale, they are scarcely more than a chapter-heading, and their mediocrity is forgotten in the very real excellence of the narrative as a whole.

It is on this basis, partly, that one can presume to excuse Crabbe's most famous "bad" lines. In 1812 appeared *Rejected Addresses*, by James and Horace Smith, consisting of a delightful set of parodies of the most popular poets of the day in the form of addresses supposedly rejected by the committee which was to procure a prologue to celebrate the opening of the Drury Lane Theatre after it had burned in 1809. The parody of Crabbe, "The Theatre," was generally acclaimed as one of the most successful. He himself was not displeased, and wrote to a friend: "You were more feeling than I was, when you read the excellent parodies of the young men who wrote the 'Rejected Addresses.' There is a little ill-nature—and, I take the liberty of adding, undeserved ill-nature—in their prefatory address; but in their versification, they have done me admirably. They are extraordinary men; but it is easier to imitate style, than to furnish matter."[25]

For our purposes, the most interesting part of the publication is the notes, which in the case of Crabbe must have been added after 1819, as will presently appear. It is in these notes, incidentally, that the epithet "Pope in worsted stockings" first appears, to haunt all succeeding critics of Crabbe;[26] certainly the verses which the Smiths composed were sufficiently in accord with their own designation of the poet:

> John Richard William Alexander Dwyer
> Was footman to Justinian Stubbs, Esquire;
> But when John Dwyer listed in the Blues,
> Emanuel Jennings polish'd Stubbs's shoes.
> Emanuel Jennings brought his youngest boy
> Up as a corn-cutter—a safe employ.[27]

In the notes to the parody of Crabbe, the Smiths relate an anecdote about the writer's first interview with the poet, how he appeared to have forgotten a passage from his own poetry, and conclude with the following:

It is not a little extraordinary that Crabbe, who could write with such vigour, should descend to such lines as the following:—

> "Something had happen'd wrong about a bill
> Which was not drawn with true mercantile skill;

[25] *Life*, p. 275.

[26] Lockhart emended this to "Dryden in a one-horse chaise;" see *Quarterly Review*, vol. LII (1834), p. 185.

[27] *Rejected Addresses*, 18th edition, London, 1833, p. 144.

> So, to amend it, I was told to go
> And seek the firm of Clutterbuck and Co."

Surely "Emanuel Jennings," compared with the above, rises to sublimity.[28]

Now these lines are sadly misquoted, a fact which seems hitherto not to have been noticed, and since some critics seem to have read the Smiths rather than Crabbe, I think the true version, though assuredly no great improvement, should be recorded:

> "Something one day occur'd about a bill
> "That was not drawn with true mercantile skill,
> "And I was ask'd and authorized to go
> "To seek the firm of Clutterbuck and Co.
>
> [*Tales of the Hall* VII, 470–473.]

When one is faced with such an appalling passage, there may be reason to be suspicious of one's own shock as much as of the verse itself. If ever before or since in the history of English poetry the abbreviation "Co." had been made to rhyme with "go" we might accept the passage as incredibly bad and hurry on to something else, but surely a poet does not resort to something like this without a reason. If we look at the tale as a whole, at the character of the Elder Brother of *Tales of the Hall* who tells the story, and at the immediate context of the passage, some new meanings seem to appear which, to my mind, justify the outlandish rhyme, and even give it significance.

As we may recall from the brief discussion in the previous essay, the Elder Brother, George, has been a "romantic," who to dream his dreams

> ". . . chose a woody scene,
> "My guardian-shade, the world and me between;
> "A green inclosure, where beside its bound
> "A thorny fence beset its beauties round,
> "Save where some creature's force had made a way
> "For me to pass, and in my kingdom stray.
>
> [*Tales of the Hall* VII, 130–136.]

28 *Ibid.*, p. 136.

George has a hopeless love affair, then is persuaded by his wealthy uncle to enter trade with him. He says of the uncle:

> "He, the most saving of mankind, had still
> "Some kindred feeling; he would guide my will,
> "And teach me wisdom—so affection wrought,
> "That he to save me from destruction sought:
> "To him destruction, the most awful curse
> "Of misery's children, was—an empty purse!
>
> [*Ibid.* 381–386.]

Later, after the dénouement of the love affair, to which the "Clutterbuck" passage leads, he says:

> 'I now could talk and scheme with *men of sense*
> "Who deal for millions, and who sigh for pence;
> "And grew so like them, that I heard with joy
> "Old Blueskin said I was a pretty boy;
> "For I possess'd the caution, with the zeal,
> "That all true lovers of their interest feel.
> "Exalted praise! and to the creature due
> "Who loves that interest solely to pursue.
>   "But I was sick, and sickness brought disgust;
> "My peace I could not to my profits trust . . .
>
> [*Ibid.* 803–811.]

This seems to make quite clear the attitude which George, as a fictional character, took toward business and trade. That it also reflects Crabbe's own attitude may not be entirely beside the point.[29] Keeping this in mind, let us now place the Clutterbuck passage in context:

> ". . . not contented, not in discontent,
> "As my good uncle counsell'd, on I went;
> "Conscious of youth's great error—nay, the crime
> "Of manhood now—a dreary waste of time!

---

[29] See the description of a dream found in Crabbe's 1817 London Journal under the date of July 21: ". . . Awake, I had been with the high, the apparently happy: we were very pleasantly engaged, and my last thoughts were cheerful. Asleep, all was misery and degradation, not my own only, but of those who had been.—That horrible image of servility and baseness—that mercenary and commercial manner! . . ." (*Life*, p. 241).

"Conscious of that account which I must give
"How life had past with me—I strove to live.
   "Had I, like others, my first hope attain'd,
"I must, at least, a certainty have gain'd;
"Had I, like others, lost the hope of youth,
"Another hope had promised greater truth;
"But I in baseless hopes, and groundless views,
"Was fated time, and peace, and health to lose,
"Impell'd to seek, for ever doom'd to fail,
"Is—I distress you—let me end my tale.
   "Something one day occurr'd about a bill
"That was not drawn with true mercantile skill,
"And I was ask'd and authorized to go
"To seek the firm of Clutterbuck and Co.;

[*Ibid.*, 456–473.]

Keeping in mind that a carefully conceived character is supposed to be reciting this tale, the contrast, the change of mood
between the first part of the entire passage and the Clutterbuck
lines scarcely needs to be pointed out. The speaker has broken
off the action of the story to relapse into his own, somewhat
ironic, musings, to return again briefly to the feelings which
he endured at the time that action occurred; but suddenly he
catches himself, and plunges into the matter of his tale. As he
makes the change from musing to action, however, all the bitterness he felt against his commercial environment suddenly
crystallizes, and the ridiculous, and intentionally ridiculous,
Clutterbuck rhyme emerges. The line "That was not drawn
with true mercantile skill," with the false rhythm,[30] and the
"ask'd and authorized" in the next line (which, note, the Smiths
left out of their misquotation), cannot by accident place so
much emphasis on the commercial jargon which George de-
spises, and as a final, satiric statement of his opinion on that
jargon and on the whole world which it represents there is the
"Clutterbuck and Co." rhyme.

[30] *N.E.D.* cites this line as an illustration of "of or proper to a merchant."
No pronunciation of "mercantile" other than that with accent on the first syllable
is given.

This discussion has been intended merely to indicate that we must not be too casual in condemning Crabbe's "bad" lines, which is particularly true since he so frequently writes with obviously conscious and intentional humor. I do not mean to suggest that we can pick random "bad" lines from Crabbe and in every case defend them, although, as should now be clear, we might always do well to pause before finally deciding how "bad" a line actually is. But the trouble with Crabbe's verse is that we can never be altogether sure of the poet, for there can be no doubt that Saintsbury's objections have a basis in fact. Dryden, Pope, or Johnson would not have allowed lines like the "Jachin" couplet to stand, nor can we believe that a poet with an extremely sensitive ear would have been apt to do so, since the badness of these lines serves, as such, no possible function in the context. Yet there they are.

But it is possible that Crabbe's lack of care in regard to the versification of his later works has been overstressed, even by the modest poet himself. The couplet is much more pliant and relaxed in *Tales of the Hall* than in *The Village,* but then the poet was not trying to do the same thing with it, and what appeared at the time as carelessness to critics whose ears were attuned to more strictly Popian verse, may well have been the result of deliberate intention, or at least of an unconscious and intuitive adaptation of the verse to the matter. That Crabbe took some care in revision is indicated by a letter to Miss Charter: ". . . I cannot be in Town while you are there . . . My journey is prevented by several Circumstances; I cannot yet prepare my new, and (most assuredly), my last Work for the Press: the Correction takes more Time than I know how to spare: my Head can bear but a little at a time . . . to say the Truth I am weary of reading, writing, and Correcting Verses."[31] He was no doubt weary of revision, but he did revise. Kebbel reports of the fact that Crabbe's versification seemed to show

[31] Broadley and Jerrold, p. 207. The letter is dated April 15, 1818. *Tales of the Hall* was published in July, 1819, "after four years of labour, and of late almost incessant . . ." (*Huchon,* p. 406, note, quoted from a letter of Crabbe to his publisher Murray. Huchon does not make the date of this letter clear, but it may be 22 January 1819.)

evidences of less care in his old age: "When asked by Rogers what was the reason for this difference, Crabbe very candidly replied that in his youthful composition he was on his promotion, but that when his popularity was assured, he no longer felt it necessary to take so much trouble. No real lover of style as such would ever have given this reply."[32]

This is probably true, and I think no one would propose Crabbe as a real lover of style; it is possible, however, that Crabbe simply wanted to avoid an argument with Rogers as to the merits of the style which he was then employing. Canon Ainger may indicate an answer to Kebbel's objection:

This is of course very sad, and as has already been urged, Crabbe's earlier works had the advantage of much criticism, and even correction from his friends. But, however this may be, it may fairly be urged that in a "downright" painter of human life, with that passion for realism which Crabbe was one of the first to bring back into our literature, mere "polish" would have hindered, not helped the effects he was bent on producing. It is difficult in polishing the heroic couplet not to produce the impression of seeking epigrammatic point. In Crabbe's strenuous and merciless analyses of human character his power would have been often weakened, had attention been diverted from the whole to the parts, and from the matter to the manner. The "finish" of Gray, Goldsmith, and Rogers suited exquisitely with their pensive musings on Human Life. It was otherwise with the stern presentment of such stories of human sin and misery as *Edward Shore* or *Delay has Danger*.[33]

Perhaps a Quarterly Reviewer may have the final word so far as Crabbe's mechanical defects are concerned. Writing in 1901 Mr. Heathcote Statham said: "But we maintain that Crabbe's weaknesses, as regards their quantity at all events, have been greatly exaggerated. In Shelley's complete works, the proportion of writing which is not worthy of Shelley at his best is much greater than the proportion of Crabbe which is below his best; yet no one objects to a complete edition of Shelley."[34]

[32] T. E. Kebbel, *The Life of George Crabbe*, London, 1888, p. 148.

[33] Ainger, p. 182.

[34] *Quarterly Review*, vol. CXCIII (1901), p. 43.

3

More than in the case of most poets the things we can, and must, say about Crabbe tend to cancel out one another. He wrote splendid passages of nature poetry, yet he was not a nature-poet; his best work was done in verse narrative, yet as a story-teller he has only moderate abilities; he can write passages of verse of which no poet need be ashamed, yet he can also be embarrassingly awkward and careless; his minute observation and recording of the world in front of him can be a source of great delight to readers of his verse, yet this tendency to minuteness can get out of control and result in dull cataloguing. What are we to say when faced with these facts? Is Crabbe a mere nullity because his virtues and defects nearly balance one another? I think not; by all means not. A combination of good narrative, clear and minute observation, excellent nature passages, and verse which is sometimes excellent, very seldom actually bad, and almost always thoroughly competent is a rare one, and this combination is to be found in all of Crabbe's best work. Add to this a searching and unerring psychological insight, and a poet emerges whose acquaintance is worth making, and who, once known, will not soon be forgotten. Mr. Looker remarks:

Familiarity breeds great affection for Crabbe; this is one of the outstanding things about his poetry. The permanent delight which discerning readers come to find in Crabbe—even readers who have been nourished on the great Romantic poets feel it in time—is the result of his gradual and patient investigation of motive, the development of conscience, and the growth of character. These things are at the root of his charm. Crabbe's poetry is always a criticism of life, and especially of conduct. Conduct, as Matthew Arnold said rather pompously, is three-fourths of life. The discussion of conduct and its analysis is largely the business of the novelist. It is the method of Crabbe in his narratives. This is where he joins hands across a century with the modern writers of prose fiction.[35]

[35] Looker, "In Praise of Crabbe," p. 494.

This comes very close to a statement of what I conceive to be the essential interest of Crabbe's poetry, yet the puzzle of one's enjoyment of Crabbe is not solved. Motive, conscience, and character are not enough in themselves to explain the attention of any "Romantic" to Crabbe's sobriety.

Mr. Looker has omitted one point which is of the last importance if we are to understand Crabbe, or, of perhaps more general interest, to understand why we may enjoy his works. Readers who seek only a sensuous or emotional titillation from poetry will probably in any case turn with distaste from Crabbe's serious criticism of life and from his sometimes grey-toned and always patient, his perceptive but forgiving explorations into the complexities of human living. But Mr. Whitby affirms that "his greatest quality, in virtue of which, if at all, he merits the title of poet, is his power of suggesting the infinite potentialities, for good or evil, in the humblest and obscurest lives;"[36] there is in this poetry, somehow, the suggestiveness which all great poetry possesses, which is one of the qualities of poetry.

I would propose that this poetry is to us suggestive, that it can, as we know Crabbe expected it to do, connect us, "without degradation, even to the most miserable and guilty of our fellow-men,"[37] and, so connecting us, make us see at times ranges of humanity which we seldom explore, because his works are universally and often explicitly expressive of that system of ethics which is at the root of our Western culture and to which, whether we will or no, we owe allegiance. His works are universally informed by the Christian view of the world, and if we are to appreciate, or even understand them we must accept that view as a basis for judgment. The theme of Christian resignation, as it appears, for example, in "Ellen Orford," is often not only the organizing nucleus, but also in itself the point of the tale—a point which is not made by citations of theology, nor by overt argument, but by subsuming these in the larger struc-

---

[36] Charles Whitby, "A Student of Humanity," *Poetry Review*, vol. XII (1921), p. 258.

[37] "Preface" to *The Borough*, Ward, vol. I, p. 280. See also the first essay in this volume.

ture of his belief. "Human life is everywhere a state in which much is to be endured and little to be enjoyed" is an idea with which the texture of his thought was impregnated, and which finds its reflection everywhere in Crabbe's stories. The "Golden Rule" of Christianity is the only answer possible, the only means within the limitations of men to mitigate the general suffering.

The fact that we may not like that "lesson" is no more reason to discredit the work of art in which it is found than the fact that we do not like Burtonian "melancholy" would be to discredit the dramas of John Ford, or the fact that we do not like Freudian psychology would be to discredit half of contemporary literature—but this particular "lesson" is ingrained into our very marrow, and the question of "liking" is impertinent. *Sub specie æternitatis,* one world view is about as apt to embody ultimate truth as another, and though we may justly protest that we are living in Time, not Eternity, that is the deficiency of which the honest critic must be most aware. Crabbe's expression of his view does not in itself make him a great poet, or even a poet; but, since he is a poet, it may give him a significance in the context of our culture, because it means that he has at least had it within his reach to touch something which to us is universal, and which can, for us, lift his characters for a moment from the restriction of their own little worlds to that plane where, though not losing their individuality, they become representatives of universal human attributes.

Crabbe's world view alone, of course, just as it does not make him a poet, does not make him an interesting poet. Probably most of the dullest poets in English literature partook as profoundly of Christian ethics as did Crabbe, and this in itself has but little enlivened their work. We have already noted the idea that Crabbe is entitled to the name of poet because of the quality of suggestiveness that we feel so strongly in his work, a quality which exercises its most profound appeal, I believe, because it is in his case so strongly allied with the dominating ethic of our culture. But something must come between to link the suggestiveness to the appeal, indeed to make the suggestiveness possible at all; this is the fact that unlike so many more overtly "Christian" poets Crabbe did see life steadily and, within certain limitations, whole. In his person he was by no means the bumpkin which Leslie Stephen tried to make out. A man who was born almost a peasant, but who dined with Johnson, Burke, and Reynolds and was chaplain to a duke; who served most of his life in country parsonages, but who was received in Holland House as an equal by the most glittering society of the capital; who was parochial by training and inclination, but who late in life pondered the problems of industrialization which still are not solved; who barely escaped debtors' prison, but who was forty years later a magistrate—this man is one who has had the opportunity to observe almost every condition of mankind as it falls within the ken of our society. If he is at the same time one who combines sympathetic charity with keen and unsentimental perception, and if he is so detached as to perceive relations and incongruities hidden to the individual who is irretrievably involved in the moil which he observes; if he does not fail to be aware of the humor which may alone make that confusion endurable; this is a man who is prepared by temperament to generalize upon the state of man, and to embody those generalizations in the suggestiveness of poetry.

Crabbe's Christian ethic, then, works its suggestive power by the fact that the people whom he presents become, in his hands, generalizations. The individuality of the characters in his tales has always been emphasized, and rightly so; but this is a quality not ordinarily associated with the satiric tradition in which Crabbe worked, and one which might even seem to contradict his position as a nineteenth-century representative of that tradition. What has not been sufficiently observed, and what affirms the Juvenalian cast of Crabbe's mind, is that those characters, without losing their fictional reality, become general comments upon humanity. Poor Jachin, the parish clerk who loses his soul for a shilling, is in Crabbe's hands the universal type of a man tempted and fallen into petty crime; Peter Grimes assumes an almost allegorical shape of Sin and Remorse; Sir Owen Dale re-enacts in large the results of frustrated passion which none can deny having felt in less imposing measure. The list could be extended through the roster of persons whom we meet in the poet's stories.

Santayana has remarked, in *Obiter Scripta*, "Indeed the truth is a great cathartic and wonderfully relieves the vital distress of existence. We stand as on a mountain-top, and the spectacle, so out of scale with all our petty troubles, silences and over-powers the heart, expanding it for a moment into boundless sympathy with the universe." This is the truth of generality, the kind of truth that Crabbe's poetry, at its best, possesses. This is the reason why Crabbe can be re-read, and why Saints-bury was willing to allow him greatness. That he is not among the greatest authors in English is due to occasional defects in technique and taste; he will remain secure among the consider-able figures who form a second rank of poetry, and to whom the common reader (if, as Mrs. Woolf doubted, he exists to-day) may gratefully return for instruction and delight.

BIBLIOGRAPHY

The following bibliography is a list only of those items dealing at significant length with Crabbe which I was actually able to consult in the preparation of this book. Several items I have not seen are separately listed. It would be impossible to list all the background material I have used. Where I have quoted, or have been aware of significant influence, I have endeavored to give acknowledgment in the notes.

Editions of Crabbe's poetry present no problem. The A. W. Ward edition (3 vols., Cambridge, 1905–1907) has established a standard text for all poems known up to 1900. *New Poems by George Crabbe* (edited by Arthur Pollard, Liverpool University Press, 1960) has added some fourteen poems to those previously known, but has hardly changed our view of Crabbe. The Ward edition provides a bibliography of Crabbe's poems to 1905.

ABRAMS, MEYER H.: *The Milk of Paradise*. The Effect of Opium Visions on the Works of DeQuincey, Crabbe, Francis Thompson, and Coleridge. Cambridge, Mass., 1934.

AINGER, ALFRED: *Crabbe* (English Men of Letters), New York, 1903.

BÄR, HORST: *George Crabbe als Epiker*. Eine Studie zur Technik seiner Verserzählungen, Leipzig, 1929.

BATDORF, FRANKLIN P.: "The Background of Crabbe's Village," *N. & Q.*, vol. 194, no. 22, p. 477 (October 29, 1949).

———: "An Unrecorded Early Anthology of Crabbe," *Studies in Bibliography*, vol. III (1950–1951), pp. 266–267.

BOYDEN, A. R.: "Masefield and Crabbe: An Affinity," *Bookman* (London). vol. 79 (December, 1930), p. 165.

BOYNTON, H. W.: "Life and Work of Crabbe," *Bookman,* vol. 23 (March, 1906), p. 49.

BRETT, R. L.: *Crabbe,* London, Longmans (Writers and Their Works, no. 75), 1956.

BROADLEY, A. M. and JERROLD, WALTER: *The Romance of an Elderly Poet:* A Hitherto unknown chapter in the life of George Crabbe revealed by his ten years' correspondence with Elizabeth Charter, 1815–1825. London, 1913.

BROMAN, WALTER E.: "Factors in Crabbe's Eminence in the Early Nineteenth Century," *Modern Philology,* vol. 51 (August, 1953), pp. 42–49.

BROWN, WALLACE CABLE: *The Triumph of Form:* A Study of the later masters of the heroic couplet, Chapel Hill, N.C., 1948.

BRUMBAUGH, THOMAS B.: "George Crabbe: An Unpublished Sermon," *N. & Q.,* N.S. vol. 8 (1961), pp. 20–21.

BRYANT, DONALD CROSS: *Edmund Burke and his Literary Friends,* Washington University Studies, N.S. no. 9, St. Louis, 1939.

BULBOUGH, GEOFFREY: "A Letter of Crabbe to Scott," *T.L.S.,* Sept. 22, 1932, p. 666. *Cf.* Webb, C. C. J., *ibid.,* Sept. 29, 1932, p. 691.

CAMPBELL, A. J.: "George Crabbe, Poet and Botanist," *Holborn Review,* April, 1923, p. 198.

CHAMBERLAIN, ROBERT L.: "George Crabbe and Darwin's Amorous Plants," *J.E.G.P.,* vol. 61 (October, 1962), pp. 833–852.

CHAPMAN, E. M.: "Dawn of the New Day," *English Literature in Account with Religion,* New York, 1910.

CLODD, EDWARD: *George Crabbe: A Biography,* Aldeburgh, 1865.

COLLINS, JOHN CHURTON: "The Poetry of Crabbe," *Fortnightly,* vol. 88 (October, 1907), p. 575.

[CRABBE, GEORGE]: "Biographical Account of the Rev. George Crabbe, L.L.B." *The New Monthly Magazine,* vol. 4, no. 24 (Jan. 1, 1816), p. 511.

——: *Posthumous Sermons,* ed. John D. Hastings, London, 1850.

——: *Sermons,* unpublished holograph manuscript, University of Chicago MS 639.

CRABBE, GEORGE (son): *The Life of George Crabbe,* by his Son, with an introduction by E. M. Forster, London, Oxford World's Classics, 1932. The same, with an introduction (but no index) by Edmund Blunden, London, The Cresset Press, 1947.

DAVENPORT, WILLIAM H.: "An Uncollected Poem by George Crabbe," *N. & Q.*, vol. 175 (December 31, 1938), p. 471.

DRAPER, JOHN W.: "The Metrical Tale in XVIII-Century England," *PMLA*, vol. 52 (1937), p. 390.

DUNCAN-JONES, E. E.: "Jane Austen and Crabbe," *Review of English Studies*, N.S. 5 (April, 1954), p. 174.

ELTON, OLIVER: "The Poetry of Crabbe," *Blackwoods*, vol. 185 (January, 1909), p. 78.

EVANS, J. H.: *The Poems of George Crabbe*, A Literary and Historical Study, London, 1933.

FITZGERALD, EDWARDS :"Introduction to Readings in Crabbe," *Letters and Literary Remains*, vol. VII, London, 1903.

FORSTER, E. M.: "Crabbe on Smugglers; an unpublished letter," *Spectator*, vol. 148 (Feb. 20, 1932), p. 245.

———: "George Crabbe," *Spectator*, vol. 148 (Feb. 20, 1932), p. 243.

[GIFFORD, WILLIAM]: Review of "The Borough," *Quarterly Review*, vol. 4 (November, 1810), p. 281.

GILFILLAN, GEORGE: *A Second Gallery of Literary Portraits*, Edinburgh, 1850.

GLOVER, T. R.: "Crabbe," *Poets and Puritans*, London, 1915.

GRIERSON, H. J. C.: "Scott, Shelley, and Crabbe," *T.L.S.*, September 15, 1932, p. 643.

HADDAKIN, LILIAN: *The Poetry of Crabbe*, London, Chatto & Windus, 1955.

HAZLITT, WILLIAM: *Works*, ed. P. P. Howe, London, 1930. Vol V, "Lectures on the English Poets;" vol. IX, "Critical List of Authors," from "Select British Poets"; vol. XI, "The Spirit of the Age;" vol. XIX, "Literary Criticism."

HEINLEIN, HANS: *Die Sozialen Anschauungen George Crabbes nach seinen Werken im zeitgeschichtlichen Zusammenhang dargestellt*, Kalbmünz, 1935.

HOLME, J. W.: "Treatment of Nature in Crabbe," *Primitiae: Essays in English Literature*, By Students of the University of Liverpool, Liverpool, 1912.

HUCHON, RENÉ: *George Crabbe and his Times, 1754–1832:* A Critical and Biographical Study (trans. Frederick Clarke, M.A.), London, 1907.

HUMPHREYS, ARTHUR L.: *Piccadilly Bookman,* Memorials of the House of Hatchard, London, 1893.

HUNT, LEIGH: *The Feast of the Poets,* London, 1815.

HUTTON, W. H.: "Some Memories of Crabbe," *Cornhill Magazine,* vol. 83 (June, 1901), p. 750.

JEFFREY, FRANCIS: *Contributions to the Edinburgh Review,* London, 1846.

KEBBEL, T. E.: *The Life of George Crabbe,* London, 1888.

KELLNER, KARL: *George Crabbe und seine Stellung zu den sozialen Ergebnissen der Englischen Industrie-Revolution,* Göttingen, 1935.

LANDOR, WALTER SAVAGE: *Imaginary Conversations,* ed. Charles Crump, London, 1891, vol. III.

LANG, VARLEY HOWE: "Crabbe and the 18th Century," *E.L.H.,* vol. 5, no. 4 (December, 1938).

————: "Crabbe and Tess of the D'Urbervilles," *M.L.N.,* vol. 53 (May, 1938), p. 369.

————: "Some Aspects of George Crabbe's Realism," unpublished dissertation, Johns Hopkins University, Baltimore, 1938.

LEADBEATER, MARY: *The Leadbeater Papers . . .* and the correspondence of . . . Rev. George Crabbe with Mary Leadbeater, London, 1862, vol. II.

LEAVIS, F. R.: *Revaluation:* Tradition and Development in English Poetry, New York, George W. Stewart, 1947.

LOCKHART, J. G.: "The Life and Poems of Crabbe," *Quarterly Review,* vol. 50 (1834), p. 468.

————: "Crabbe's Posthumous Tales," *Quarterly Review,* vol. 52 (1834), p. 184.

LOOKER, S. J.: "In Praise of Crabbe," *The Nineteenth Century and After,* vol. 110 (October, 1931), p. 489.

LUCAS, F. L.: "The Poet of Prose," *Life and Letters,* vol. 6 (Feb., 1931), p. 79.

MACAULAY, G. C.: Review of Vol. XI of *The Cambridge History of English Literature, M.L.R.,* vol. 11 (1916), p. 82.

MANTZ, HAROLD E.: "Non-Dramatic Pastoral in Europe in the Eighteenth Century," *PMLA,* vol. 31 (1916), p. 421.

MASSINGHAM, H. J.: *Untrodden Ways.* Adventures among the works of Hudson, Crabbe, etc., London, 1923.

MORE, PAUL ELMER: "Genius of Crabbe," *Shelburn Essays*, 2nd Series, New York, 1907.

——: "A Plea for Crabbe," *Atlantic Monthly*, vol. 88 (1901), p. 850.

OTTLEY, MAY: "George Crabbe, Dec. 24, 1754—Feb. 3, 1832," *London Mercury*, vol. 26 (June, 1932), p. 153.

PATTON, JULIA: *The English Village*, a Literary Study, 1750–1850. New York, 1919.

PAYEN, P.: "Crabbe Centenary," *Bookman*, vol. 81 (March, 1932), p. 309.

POLLARD, ARTHUR: "Two New Letters of Crabbe," *Review of English Studies*, N.S. 2 (October, 1951), pp. 375–377.

RICHARDS, F.: "George Crabbe," *London Quarterly and Holborn Review*, vol. 158 (January, 1933), p. 38.

SAINTSBURY, GEORGE: *Essays in English Literature, 1780–1860*, London, 1895.

SHEPHERD, T. N.: "George Crabbe and Methodism," *London Quarterly Review*, vcl. 166 (April, 1941), p. 166.

SHORTER, CLEMENT K.: *Immortal Memories*, New York, 1907.

SPINGARN, LAURENCE P.: "George Crabbe as Realist," *The University of Kansas City Review*, vol. 17, no. 1 (Autumn, 1950), p. 60.

STATHAM, HEATHCOTE: "Crabbe," *Quarterly Review*, vol. 193 (January, 1901), p. 21.

STEPHEN, SIR LESLIE: "Crabbe," *Hours in a Library*, series 2, London, 1876.

——: *English Literature and Society in the Eighteenth Century*, New York, 1904.

STONIER, G. W.: "Anthologies and Crabbe," *New Statesman and Nation*, vol. 27 (January 1, 1944), p. 11.

STRANG, WILLIAM: *George Crabbe*, The Quain Essay, London, 1913.

TALFOURD, SIR THOMAS NOON: "A Sketch of the History of Poetry: Crabbe," *Pamphleteer*, vol. 5 (1815), p. 437.

THALE, ROSE MARIE: "Crabbe's *Village* and Topographical Poetry," *J.E.G.P.*, vol. 55 (October, 1956), pp. 618–623.

WALPOLE, SIR SPENCER: *Essays Political and Biographical*, New York, 1908.

WECTER, DIXON: "Four Letters from George Crabbe to Edmund Burke," *R.E.S.*, vol. 14 (July, 1938), p. 298.

WHITBY, CHARLES: "A Student of Humanity," *Poetry Review,* vol. 12 (1921), p. 251.

WOHLGEMUTH, J.: *Der Stil in George Crabbe's Dichtungen,* Würzburg, 1910.

WOODBERRY, G. E.: "A Neglected Poet," *Studies in Letters and Life,* Boston, 1889.

WYLIE, L. J.: "The England of George Crabbe," *Social Studies in English Literature,* New York, 1916.

ANONYMOUS: Review of the "Life and Poems," *Edinburgh Review,* vol. 60, no. 121 (January, 1835), p. 255.

ANONYMOUS: "Commemoration of Crabbe," *Living Age,* vol. 247 (21 October 1905), p. 79.

ANONYMOUS: "A New Study of Crabbe," *Nation,* vol. 84 (23 May 1907), p. 476.

ANONYMOUS: "Non-couplet poetry of Crabbe," *Spectator,* vol. 112 (14 March 1914), p. 426.

ANONYMOUS: "George Crabbe," *T.L.S.,* 4 February 1932, p. 65.

The following items I have not consulted though they may be of interest:

BRANSBY, JAMES H.: *Brief Notices of the Late Rev. G. Crabbe in a letter to the editor of the Carnarvon Herald,* Carnarvon, 1832.

FOAKES-JACKSON, CANON F. J.: *George Crabbe,* London, 1914.

GRIBBLE, F.: "Crabbe's Aldeburgh," *Literature,* 28 September 1901.

GROVES, J.: "Crabbe as a Botanist," *Proceedings of the Suffolk Institute of Archaeology and Natural History,* vol. 12, part 2, 1905.

SALE, ARTHUR: "The Development of Crabbe's Narrative Art," *The Cambridge Journal,* vol. 5 (1952), pp. 480–98.

THOMAS, W. K.: "The Flavour of Crabbe," *The Dalhousie Review,* vol. 40 (1961) pp. 489–504.

INDEX

OLIVER SIGWORTH was born in Glendale, Arizona and educated in Arizona schools. He attended the University of Southern California, served in the U.S. Army from 1943 to 1946 and received his master's and doctor's degrees from the University of California at Berkeley. He taught at the University of California, the University of Nevada, and San Francisco State College before 1953 when he joined the English faculty at the University of Arizona. He is now an associate professor.

In 1955 the author received a grant from the Foundation for the Advancement of Education (Ford) to study eighteenth-century architecture and taste in the British Isles. Subsequently Mr. Sigworth's small volume based on his study, *Four Styles of a Decade, 1740–50*, was published by the New York Public Library. He spent a year of sabbatical leave (1962–63) at the British Museum in London doing research for a book on William Collins being published this year by Twayne. The author is also a frequent contributor to literary journals.

This book was designed by Charles McClatchy Goetz. The text was typeset in Linotype Baskerville and printed by The University of Chicago Printing Department on Warren's Olde Style text stock. The book is bound in Interlaken Pallium Linen.